Corn
Teashop Walks

Jean Patefield

COUNTRYSIDE BOOKS
NEWBURY BERKSHIRE

- COUNTRYSIDE BOOKS
3 Catherine Road
Newbury, Berkshire

To view our complete range of books,
please visit us at
www.contrysidebooks.co.uk

ISBN 1 85306 774 1

Designed by Graham Whiteman
Maps and photographs by the author

Produced through MRM Associates Ltd., Reading
Printed by J. W. Arrowsmith Ltd., Bristol

Contents

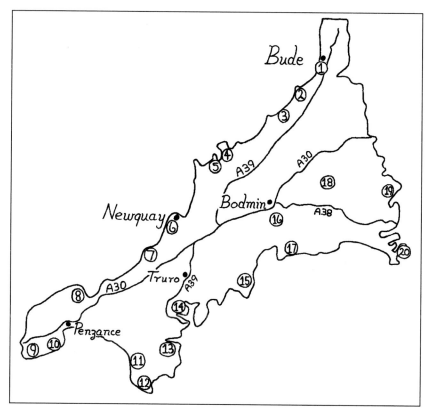

Area map showing the locations of the walks

Key to Sketch Maps

Path on route	– – –	Pub referred to in text	PH
Path not on route	. . .	Summit	△
Road	═══	Point in text	⑤
River	∿∿∿	Car park	▫
Sea	~ ~ ~	Building referred to in text	▪
Church	†		
Tea shop	☕	Quarry (disused)	⌒ᴜᴜ

Introduction

You will not need your passport or to change your currency, and in laws and constitution Cornwall is part of England; yet there is no doubt that the magical land across the Tamar is a special and different place. The river Tamar rises only four miles from the north coast and so Cornwall is almost an island.

Fortunately, much of the best of the coastline has received protection from the National Trust and the Cornwall Coastal Path makes it all accessible to the walker. Many of the routes in this book use this path to visit dramatic cliffs with outstanding vistas and fascinating geology, as well as more gentle corners.

The best teashops serve a range of cakes, all home made and including fruitcake, as well as scones and other temptations, and their teapots should be capacious and pour properly. Many of the teashops visited on these walks fulfil all these criteria admirably and they all offer a good cup of tea. They always have at least light lunches available as well so there is no need to think of these walks as just something for the afternoons.

In Cornwall there are some local specialities to enjoy. Cornish pasties were originally designed to provide miners with a complete meal, with seasoned meat, turnip, onion and potato at one end and fruit at the other. The thick, crimped edge provided a handle for arsenic-covered fingers and was discarded. Saffron cake is another Cornish speciality, dating, it is said, from the 18th and 19th centuries when England had its own thriving saffron industry.

Tea is often said to be the best meal to eat out in England and I believe it is a meal to be enjoyed on all possible occasions, and the most famous Cornish teatime treat is, of course, clotted cream served with scones and jam. It is the richest, most fattening and wickedly delicious ambrosia. Clotted cream is 12-hour-old cream that has been cooked very gently to form the semi-solid crust that is skimmed off.

There is an abundance of excellent establishments in Cornwall but even so, teashops are not scattered evenly throughout the county. In some places popular with tourists, the visitor is spoilt for choice. In such cases, the most convenient teashop that, in the author's opinion, most closely fulfils the criteria set out above is recommended, but should that not appeal, there are others from which to choose. In other places where there is a delightful walk to be enjoyed, the choice for tea is more limited. However, they all offer a good tea part way round an attractive walk. The opening times and telephone number of each teashop are given.

The pleasures of summer walking are obvious. In Cornwall spring comes early and summer lingers longer and walking outside the summer season means you are more likely to have the landscape to yourself. Be aware that many teashops are rather vague about when they open out of season: it seems to depend on weather and mood. If you are planning a walk on a wet November Tuesday, for example, a call to check that tea will actually be available that day is a wise precaution. Many are definitely closed outside the summer season and for these walks, where possible, an alternative source of refreshment is given. In most cases, these are pubs serving food, which sometimes includes tea.

The twenty walks in this book explore the varied landscapes of Cornwall. They are all between three and seven and a half miles long and should be well within the capacity of the average person, including those of mature years and families with children. They are intended to take the walker through this attractive corner of England at a gentle pace with plenty of time to stop and stare, to savour the beauty and interest all around. A dedicated yomper and stomper could probably knock off the whole book in a single weekend but in doing so they would have missed the point and seen nothing. To fully appreciate the countryside it is necessary to go slowly with your eyes and ears open.

Some of the walks are short and level, ideal for a pipe opener on a winter's day, or giving plenty of time to dawdle away a summer's afternoon. Others are longer or more strenuous, some making an excellent all-day expedition. Certain of the walks involve some climbing. This is inevitable as the undulations of cliffs add enormous interest, and with no ascents, there are no views. However, this presents no problem to the sensible walker who has three uphill gears – slowly, very slowly and admiring the view.

All the routes are on public rights of way or permissive paths and have been carefully checked but, of course, in the countryside things do change; a stile replaces a gate or a wood is extended. A sketch map illustrates each walk and all except two are circular. An

Ordnance Survey map is useful as well, especially for identifying the main features of views. The Explorer 1:25,000 (2½ inches to 1 mile) series are by far the best maps to use for walking. Sheets 102 to 109 inclusive cover Cornwall. The grid reference of the starting point and the appropriate maps are given for each walk.

Of course, it behoves us all to remember that the place where we take our recreation is other people's workplace and act with consideration to those who depend on the countryside for their livelihood and make their homes there.

Nevertheless, a right of way is exactly what it says – it gives a right of passage over what is otherwise private land. Landowners are not allowed to block a right of way but agricultural activities such as ploughing and harvesting sometimes of necessity obliterate footpaths and this is legal providing the path is restored within two weeks. Many farmers are conscientious about this and even where they are not, the walkers' feet will do the job on a well-used path. Problems can arise when a farmer does not restore a little used path and crops grow up across the line. What is the walker to do? To walk round the edge of the field is technically a trespass and anyway is not always as easy as it sounds. The alternative is to keep to the line of the path and trample down the crops. This is what the law requires you to do, providing no more damage than absolutely necessary is caused, and yet this course of action often doesn't feel right. The solution in each case is a matter of common sense, but it is always worth remembering when walking in the countryside that a right of way is not a concession but a prerogative and that footpaths and bridleways are part of this country's highway network.

The walks, all starting at a car park, are designed so that the teashop is reached in the second half so a really good appetite for tea can be worked up and then its effects walked off. However, it sometimes fits in better with the plans for the day to start and finish at the teashop and so for each walk there are details of how to do this.

So put on your walking shoes and prepare to be delighted by the charms of Cornwall and refreshed by a traditional English tea!

Jean Patefield

Walk 1
BUDE

*M*ost *of this walk is beside water – but what a contrast! The outward leg is along the cliffs beside the turbulent Atlantic, which eats away at the rock exposing the interesting geology. Associated with this are the downs and ups that cliff walking brings. The return leg is along a level, surfaced path beside a historic canal studded with water lilies. These two elements are connected by a permissive path granted by Whaleborough Farm, which gives easier access to the coast than the right of way.*

The Castle Tea Room in Bude offers a delicious selection of home-made cakes including, on my visit, biennestick, which is a light sponge with vanilla cream and topped with almonds. Cream teas are served as well, of course. For lunch there is a good choice of sandwiches, salads and filled jacket potatoes. In addition to the usual ploughman's lunch there is a range of variations on the theme, such as Frenchman's lunch with pâté and pigman's lunch with pork sausages. There is plenty of seating inside, where you can inspect the work of local artists, as well as tables outside. The teashop is open every day from just before Easter until late October between 10 am and 5 pm. Telephone: 01288 355734.

There are, of course, a multitude of teashops and other refreshment places of all sorts in Bude, but also particularly worthy of mention is Woodland Tea Garden at the start of the walk. Telephone: 01288 361015.

DISTANCE: 5½ miles.

MAP: OS Explorer 111 Bude, Boscastle and Tintagel.

STARTING POINT: Helebridge car park (GR 216036).

HOW TO GET THERE: From the A39, Bude-Wadebridge road, about a mile and a half south of Bude, take a minor road, Helebridge Road, signed 'Marhamchurch'. Turn left immediately into Hele Road to a small, unsigned car park on the right next to Wharf Cottage.

ALTERNATIVE STARTING POINT: If you wish to visit the teashop at the beginning or end of your walk, start in Bude, where there are several signed car parks: there is a small one on the wharf by the canal and the next closest is the short stay car park. The teashop is on the canal wharf, towards the sea end. You will then start the walk at point 7.

THE WALK

1. Return to the main road, the A39, and cross it to take a surfaced track, which passes the Woodland Tea Garden and goes uphill.

2. Opposite a farmhouse on the right, turn left between farm buildings and continue on a surfaced track. Press on along the track when the surface ends.

3. Just before the track peters out in a field as Widemouth Bay comes into view, turn right on a less well defined track to a gate onto a road. Cross the road and go ahead to meet the coast path.

4. Turn right. Follow this for two miles to a tower on the cliffs above Bude.

The cliffs vividly illustrate the effects of earth movements on the rocks beneath our feet. The cliffs are made of layers of sandstone and shale laid down at the bottom of a shallow sea or delta 300 million years ago. As conditions changed over the millennia, slightly different sediments accumulated, producing the different

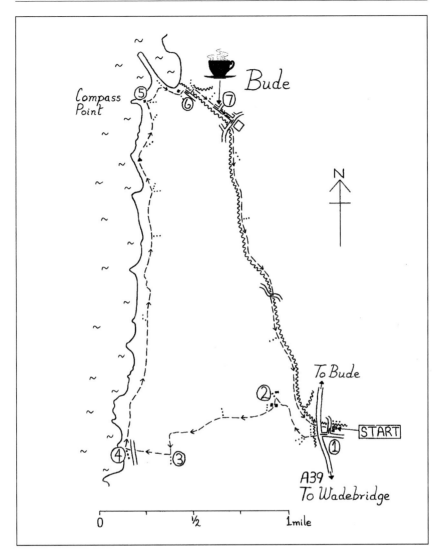

layers. *Later earth movements buckled and folded them so that in some places the layers are almost vertical. This is quite soft rock and the eroded stumps can be seen offshore at low tide. The vegetation is a mixture of grasses with flowers such as sea campion, thrift, wild carrot, heath and gorse. One interesting plant to look out for is dodder, which is a parasite on gorse and looks like red string thrown onto the plants. It bears a mass of small, pink flowers in August.*

The views from the cliff are magnificent and a topograph along the way helps you pick out the main features. The tower has the points of the compass marked on its sides and gives its name to this headland, Compass Point. It used to fly cones to warn shipping of gales. It has been dismantled once and re-erected further inland due to erosion of the cliffs.

Compass Point

5. Now bear right, still on the coast path to a gate onto a road at Efford Cottage. Turn right along the road for 50 yards.

☕ **6.** Go down some steps on the left and cross the canal at the sea gates. Across the gates turn right to the teashop on the left.

Bude Castle, now the Council offices, was built by local inventor and philanthropist Sir Goldsworthy Gurney. Among his inventions was a bizarre musical instrument consisting of glasses played as a piano. He improved the lighting in the House of Commons, replacing the 280 candles with three Bude lights, used for 60 years until the arrival of electricity. His light shone extra brightly because oxygen was injected into the flame. He adapted it for use in lighthouses by placing it in a revolving frame which caused a flashing beam. Each lighthouse had its own sequence of flashes so mariners could tell which light was which, a principle still in use today. His invention is commemorated in Bude's newest and oft-derided monument, which resembles a tall, stripey candle. It comes into its own at night when it is illuminated by fibre optics in a pattern of constellations. By the canal and teashop is the Town Museum in an old blacksmith's forge. It is open throughout the summer and has some interesting exhibits about Bude Canal.

7. Continue by the canal to a road. Cross the road to carry on beside the water, shortly passing a hide overlooking Bude Marshes. Press on along the canal-side path when it crosses the canal at the first bridge. The river joins the canal at a weir then shortly leaves it again. Take a footbridge across the river then carry on by the canal to the main road. Cross the road and the path ahead shortly leads to a lane and the car park.

Bude Canal was an ambitious, early canal project originally conceived to link the Atlantic with the English Channel by way of the Tamar. Built at a cost of £118,000 and opened in 1823, it never got further than Launceston. The main trade was taking sand, rich in calcium carbonate, to sweeten the acid soils of north-east Cornwall and north-west Devon; grain and other produce was brought the other way. Before the canal was opened, the beach was thronged with carters loading wagons and packhorses with sand. One unusual feature of the canal was that it used inclined planes to move the tub boats from one level to another. The boats were fitted with wheels so they could be hauled up ramps along metal rails. The power was provided by water, harnessed either by a water wheel driving an endless chain or by the weight of buckets laden with water descending into pits. The water was released from the buckets to run along a channel into the canal and the empty bucket was raised and refilled ready to repeat the process. The first incline was at Marhamchurch and you can see the remains by following the canal a little further. The canal went out of business in 1891 under increased competition from the railway.

Walk 2
CRACKINGTON HAVEN

This *is an exhilarating walk visiting some of the highest cliffs in Cornwall towering above Strangles beach. The views, north to Hartland Point in Devon and south to Trevose Head, are some of the best along this coast. It is difficult to appreciate at first just how high these cliffs are because the geology has led to a crumpled undercliff rather than a precipice. The walk towards Crackington Haven is fascinating, with the contorted strata in the rock and obvious erosion revealing the tremendous forces at work in nature. The return is in complete contrast, following a path up a heavily wooded and sheltered valley beside a stream. Though this walk is short it is strenuous so do not underestimate the time it might take. The valley path can be muddy and the cliff path has rough stretches so stout footwear is recommended.*

The Cabin, owned by a local farmer, prides itself on using the best of local produce. They serve a delicious selection of home-made cakes, including what is probably the best coffee and walnut cake I have ever tasted. The pasties are made from local beef and they also serve a choice of baguettes and an all-day breakfast. They are open all day, every day between Easter and the end of October and sometimes at weekends in winter if the weather is favourable. Telephone: 01840 230238.

DISTANCE: 3½ miles.
MAP: OS Explorer 111 Bude, Boscastle and Tintagel.
STARTING POINT: Strangles beach car park. (GR 134951).
HOW TO GET THERE: From the A39, Bude-Wadebridge road, about 10 miles south of Bude, take the B3263 towards Boscastle. After about 2¼ miles turn right along a lane, signed 'Trevigue' for about 1¾ miles to the second parking area on the right.
ALTERNATIVE STARTING POINT: If you wish to visit the tea shop at the beginning or end of your walk, start in Crackington Haven, where there is a car park (charge). The teashop is beside the car park. You will then start the walk at point 4.

THE WALK

1. Continue along the lane a few yards then turn left on a hedged path by the National Trust 'Strangles' sign.

Strangles is a wonderful beach and a path leading down was once used by donkeys carrying sand and slate collected from the shore. It is not difficult to go down but rather a pull coming back, so it is particularly important not to forget anything! Its relative seclusion means that it is popular with naturists and, according to reports, naturists and 'textiles' get along harmoniously. High Cliff, to the left, at 731 feet is the most elevated in Cornwall.

2. At the coast path turn right.

In the Carboniferous period, over 300 million years ago, Britain lay near the equator. Sand and mud carried by rivers were deposited on the seabed. As the rocks were carried north by the movement of the continents, pressures in the crust changed the rocks into shale and sandstone and squeezed the layers into the folds we see today. Where the sea meets the land, the waves attack the rocks, undermining the layers above, and this causes landslips. The cliff face is not vertical and ledges and platforms show where there have been slips in the past. The fissures and crevasses by the path are evidence that this process is still going on. Softer rocks, such as the muds and shales, are eroded more quickly than slightly harder ones and this produces features of the coastline such as the dramatic promontory called 'Cambeak', looking like a sleeping dinosaur.

15

☕ **3.** At a saddle point just before the obvious promontory of Cambeak the path splits into three: one goes up and round the promontory, one contours round the hillside and one goes round the bottom. They all meet further on. The one round the bottom is easiest! Continue along the coast path to Crackington Haven and the teashop, across the road.

As you walk along this coast there are several other interesting things to note. Small streams leading to the sea have carved deep valleys. The coast is eroding so fast that hanging valleys are formed and the streams cascade onto the beach as waterfalls. These little valleys are very sheltered compared with the cliffs. By the path at one point is a small copse of stunted oaks and this gives you an idea of what the vegetation would be like without human interference by grazing and deliberate clearance. The trees are stunted by the salt-laden wind off the sea. There is a much larger area of this distinctive woodland north of Crackington Haven, known as the Dizzard, but it is not open to the public.

Once a small port similar to many others along the North Cornwall coast, Crackington Haven imported limestone and coal and exported slate and local produce. In contrast to developed ports like Bude and Boscastle, Crackington Haven remained a harbour in only the most basic sense that small boats could pull up onto the beach at low tide. In the early 19th century plans were drawn up to construct a large port. A harbour and docks covering 12 acres, with a rail link to Launceston was planned and would have been called Port Victoria. Perhaps fortunately, the scheme was never realised. This remote stretch of coastline, conveniently distant from authority, was also home to smugglers and wreckers. A ridge of shingle protects the beach. People tend to take the pebbles as souvenirs, for water features or as ballast and this exposes the beach and property behind to enhanced erosion. You may see an award-winning leaflet round the village asking people not to do this.

4. Turn right out of the teashop along a track beside a stream. Immediately before a house turn right up to a lane. Turn left for 40 yards then right along a track signed 'East Wood'. Continue ahead when the track becomes a path.

5. Some 50 yards after crossing a stream at a footbridge turn right, signed 'Sheepdip', to shortly reach a second footbridge and a T-junction. Turn left. At a junction press on up the valley, still signed 'Sheepdip'.

6. At a cross path turn right, signed 'Trevigue'. On leaving the wood head straight up a field to a stile into a second field. Now bear slightly right to a gate to the right of some houses seen ahead. Through the gate carry on ahead to a lane and turn left back to the start.

Dating from the 16th century, Trevigue Farmhouse is dug into the hillside with its back to the prevailing wind. The farm is now partly owned by the National Trust and managed for conservation as well as production, an approach for which it has won several awards. The aim is to encourage the greatest biodiversity possible, and as a result the farm is home to a rich variety of wildlife, including badgers, roe deer, tawny owls, barn owls, otters, hares, four species of bat and peregrine falcons. Habitats have also been specially created on the farm for dormice, Large Blue butterflies and the rarest member of the crow family – the striking, red-legged chough.

Walk 3
BOSCASTLE

This superb walk packs more into three and a half strenuous miles than many longer walks do in twice the distance. It has a bit of everything and if someone could do only one walk in Cornwall and wanted to capture the essence, this would be the one to recommend. The countryside behind Boscastle is deeply dissected by steep-sided, wooded valleys. This route starts with a beautiful path up one such valley before a steep climb up to an ancient church. The seat in the churchyard, filled with flowers in spring, is a lovely place to rest and admire the view inland. The route then leads on to Boscastle old village, so different from the hubbub round the car park, before a second, shorter climb to another old church and a walk across a medieval field system to the coast path and some spectacular scenery. From there it's downhill all the way to the interesting old harbour and a good tea. What else could you ask for?

There are teashops all around the car park at Boscastle. The Riverside Tea Rooms has the advantage of a most attractive terrace overlooking the river. Based in a 16th-century house built by Sir Richard

Grenville, who sailed with Drake at the Armada, they serve a very good selection of home-made cakes including Cornish apple cake and, on my visit, delicious and unusual brown sugar meringues with clotted cream and fresh fruit. Another unusual item on the menu is a shortbread 'clam' also filled with clotted cream and fruit. Possibilities for lunch range from sandwiches and baguettes to full meals. They are open every day between noon and 5 pm throughout the year. Telephone: 01840 250216.

DISTANCE: 3½ miles.

MAP: OS Explorer 111 Bude, Boscastle and Tintagel.

STARTING POINT: Boscastle car park (GR 100912).

HOW TO GET THERE: Boscastle is on the B3263, signed from the A39, Bude-Wadebridge road, about ten miles south of Bude. This road passes the car park.

ALTERNATIVE STARTING POINT: This walk differs from the others in this book because the starting point is by the teashop. Parking is very limited in the Boscastle area and there is no other suitable starting point.

THE WALK

1. Go to the rear of the car park and follow the clear path up Valency Valley. Continue past stepping-stones to a footbridge.

Thomas Hardy, the author, was an architect by profession. In 1870 he was sent to St Juliot, further up the valley, to oversee the restoration of the church. He met and fell in love with Emma Gifford, the girl with 'nut brown hair, grey eyes and rose-flush coming and going'. They married in 1874 but the union turned sour. When Emma died in 1912 Hardy, consumed with remorse, wrote some lyric love poems to her memory. In one he refers to a tumbler they lost on a picnic in Valency Valley:

> By night by day, when it shines or lours,
> There lies intact that chalice of ours...

2. Turn right over the footbridge, signed 'Minster Church', and follow the path ahead up through a wood.

3. When the path forks bear left up to a track. Turn right for 70 yards then cross a stile on the right into a churchyard. Follow the path past the church and up through the churchyard to a seat well placed to admire the view and a gate onto a lane.

This has been a sacred site for at least 1,500 years. First, it was a Celtic religious cell, possibly founded by Madryn, a Welsh princess who fled her country. It then became a Benedictine monastery until 1402, when Henry IV expelled foreign monasteries. The building was rebuilt in the 16th century, probably using stone from the earlier foundation. When the roof collapsed one Sunday evening in 1869 the building was restored again, so, despite the antiquity of the site, what we see today is essentially a Victorian building. However, note the 17th-century memorials in the south-east corner. The view from the churchyard is lovely, especially in spring when it is carpeted with flowers.

4. Turn right along the lane. Ignore paths on the left and right and a lane on the left, and walk along the lane for about half a mile.

5. When the lane bends left continue in the same direction over a stone stile. Head across a field to another stile onto a stream bank. Over the stile bear right to walk along the left hand side of a small field to regain the stream bank and walk downstream a short distance. The path passes a house and crosses the stream and becomes a track. Bear left when the track forks to emerge on the old village street.

6. Turn right. A path on the right just as the street bends left leads to the site of Bottreaux Castle.

Nicholas de Bottreaux fought with William the Conqueror and built his castle on a spur overlooking the harbour. An information board tells you more. There is nothing to be seen now except the view as the site is half built over. The name lingers on in the village that grew up, well away from the wind-swept coast. Many of the buildings are charming, as the roofs sweep in graceful curves caused by warping of their timbers and settlement of the walls. Look for a cottage called 'Kiddlywink', an old Cornish name for an alehouse, apparently just one of fifteen premises in Boscastle that used to sell alcohol but which are now dry.

7. When the road forks just after a house called 'Little Glen' on the right, bear left up to a main road. Turn left then immediately right up Forrabury Hill for 50 yards. Turn right on a path signed 'To the coast path' and follow it up steeply to a gate. Through the gate continue ahead to meet a track just before a church. Turn right and follow the track round the church – there is an entrance to the churchyard a little further on – and continue ahead to the cliff path.

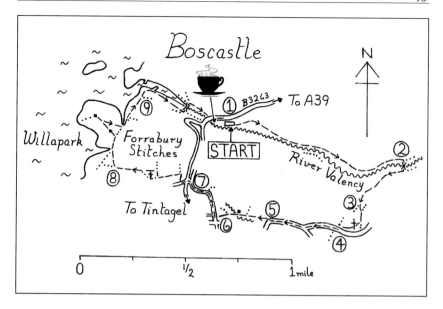

St Symphorian's is another Norman church heavily restored in Victorian times. The medieval benches were taken out as, the parish records tell us, '... the inhabitants are inconvenienced for want of sittings'. Some were used to form the pulpit, altar and credence table and their carvings can still be made out. St Symphorian is better known in his native Burgundy; he was beheaded in AD 282 for protesting against the worship of the goddess Cybele.

Forrabury Common is divided into 42 stitches, or plots, mostly owned by the National Trust. This is an ancient type of land tenure dating from Celtic times. Each plot is cultivated by its tenant from Lady Day (25 March) until Michaelmas (29 September). The plots are separated by banks instead of fences and are grazed in common for the rest of the year. This type of farming is obviously uneconomic nowadays but is maintained by the Trust because of its historic interest. In addition, the banks are home to many wild flowers that find a niche as arable weeds that modern farming has made much less common.

8. Turn right. It is well worth diverting left up the promontory, Willapark, to the building on top for the very best views. When returning down, the left branch of the path leads back to the cliff path a little further on. Continue along the cliff path until you are level with the outer breakwater of the harbour.

Boscastle Harbour seen from Willapark

The promontory of Willapark is 317 feet high and offers an unrivalled viewpoint both along the coast and inland. It was inhabited in the Iron Age and the natural advantages were enhanced by a bank and ditch across the isthmus. The white building on the summit was constructed in the early 19th century as a tea house, but you now have to go a little further for tea. It was subsequently used as a lookout.

☕ **9.** Bear left on a lower path down to the harbour. Cross the river at a footbridge and continue ahead to the teashop and the car park.

The sinuous natural inlet is the only harbour along 40 miles of dangerous coast and was important in the 19th century since the railway did not reach north Cornwall until 1893. Coal, iron and limestone from South Wales and a whole variety of goods from Bristol were the main imports, while china clay, slate and manganese from a mine in Valency Valley were the main exports. The tortuous channel and an island just offshore made it unsafe for boats to enter unassisted. They were 'hobbled' in by being towed by a boat manned by a team of eight rowers while ropes to men on the shore steadied the craft in the channel. The quay was rebuilt in 1584 under the orders of Sir Richard Grenville, High Sheriff of Cornwall. The outer breakwater was added in 1820 but blown up by a floating mine in 1941. The National Trust rebuilt it as the sea was again threatening the quay. By the harbour is a most unusual museum dedicated to witchcraft, open daily April until Halloween from 10.30am (Sunday 11.30am) until 6pm Telephone 01840 250111. It has intriguing displays such as dark mirrors that see into the future.

Walk 4
DAYMER BAY AND ROCK

*J*ohn *Betjeman loved this part of Cornwall ever since he came on holiday as a small boy and he immortalised it in his poems. He is buried at a tiny Norman church, threatened for centuries by shifting sands. This gentle walk explores the sand dunes on the eastern bank of the Camel estuary, tamed by golf links on the outward leg and in its natural state on the return, to visit a lively café at Rock, best known as a sailing centre. If the tide is out, the whole of the return can be made along an unbroken expanse of golden sand.*

The Blue Tomato is a modern establishment attractively positioned overlooking the Camel estuary facing Padstow. There is a covered terrace and the contemporary interior has picture windows so you can appreciate the view whatever the weather. This is really a place to visit for lunch, though cream teas and toasted teacakes are served. There is an innovative and tasty selection of baguettes and sandwiches and a tempting choice of daily specials ranging from ham and eggs to skate wings. The name comes from a painting, hanging in the café done by a local artist for the owner depicting a tomato plant against a blue background. In keeping, the menu includes blue tomato salad, which is tomato with dolce latte cheese. They are open 9.30 am until 6 pm from March until the end of October and 'sometimes in winter'. Telephone: 01208 863841. When the teashop is closed the Rock Inn nearby is open all year and serves food.

DISTANCE: 3 miles.

MAP: OS Explorer 106 Newquay and Padstow.

STARTING POINT: Daymer Bay car park (charge) (GR 928777).

HOW TO GET THERE: From the junction of the A39 and A389 at Wadebridge take the B3314, signed 'Polzeath Rock Port Isaac' for about 4 miles. Turn left, signed 'Trebetherick 3 Rock 2½ Pityme 1¼'. Just after the Pityme Inn on the left, turn right on Trewiston Lane, signed 'Trebetherick 1½ Polzeath 2'. Take a little lane on the left, signed 'Daymer Bay ½' to a car park (charge) at the end of the lane.

ALTERNATIVE STARTING POINT: If you wish to visit the teashop at the beginning or end of your walk, start in Rock, where there is a car park (charge) at the end of the road, just beyond The Blue Tomato. You will then start the walk at point 7.

THE WALK

1. Return to the entrance to the car park and walk back up the lane for 100 yards. Turn right on a track, signed 'Footpath to St Enodoc Church'. When the track ends continue along a path across a golf course, bearing left to the church.

St Enodoc's church dates from Norman times, though the twisted spire was added in the 13th century. It was not built among sand dunes: in those days there was a village between the church and the sea but it was overwhelmed by sand as changes in local conditions allowed the dunes to grow. In 1857 a great gale stripped the sand from twelve feet below the current high water mark and stumps of oak and yew were revealed. The church has been almost buried several times. In the early 19th century the vicar and congregation had to get in through the roof to hold the annual service required to maintain the church's rights to tithes. John Betjeman, the much-loved Poet Laureate, came to this area on holiday as a child. Fond memories of those days take up two chapters of his verse autobiography, 'Summoned by Bells', in which he recalls the excitement of arriving by train, playing on the beach with other children and this little church,

'Come on! Come on! This hillock hides the spire....'

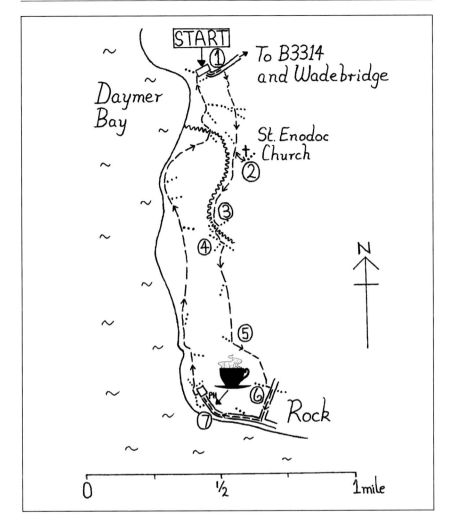

He died in 1984 at his home in Trebetherick and his grave lies to the right of the path as you face the church, beneath a simple Cornish slate headstone.

2. After looking at the church return down to the path and turn left to continue across the golf course: the path is shown by white stones.

3. At a track go ahead to the left of a stream then turn right across a brick footbridge. After 20 yards turn left to a surfaced drive.

St Petroc came to Cornwall as a missionary from Wales and is reputed to have landed at Daymer Bay before crossing the estuary to Padstow and establishing a monastery. He met a group of peasants who were hot and thirsty from their work in the fields and, in the way that saints do, he struck a rock with his staff and a stream of cool water leaped forth. The stream across the golf course is said to be St Petroc's stream.

4. Turn left. Ignore a path on the right after 10 yards and take a second after a further 20 yards, again following the line shown by the white stones, to a fence with white-topped posts.

5. Turn left in front of the fence to walk with it on your right. Follow the path as it crosses the fence and press on to a track.

☕ **6.** Turn left to a lane and then right along the lane to a T-junction. Turn right to the teashop on the right.

With so much sand about, visitors must often wonder how it came to be called Rock. The name comes from an outcrop of dark greenstone known as Black Rock or Blacktor that pokes its head out of the sand near the village. A ferry has been running between Rock and Padstow across the river since 1337 and all the ferries have been called Blacktor. Its ancient charter requires it to run from sunrise to sunset seven days a week and it still does that in summer but there is a more restricted service in winter. Today Rock is a popular centre for dinghy sailing and there is racing most weeks in the summer.

7. Turn right out of the teashop and follow the road into Rock Quarry car park. About half way along bear left onto the signed coast path. There are roughly three more or less parallel paths that thread their way through the dunes. Follow any of them, but do not stray to the right or you will end up on the golf course. Within sight of the car park the path peters out and the best way back is to turn left onto the beach and up the steps to the car park. If the tide is out, you can walk all the way back to Daymer Bay from Rock along the beach.

For more about sand dunes see Walk 8, page 43. The green mound rising in front of the church and passed as you return towards the car park is Brea Hill, the site of a Roman settlement. Roman coins and other artefacts dating from the 3rd and 4th centuries have been found in the neighbourhood.

Walk 5
STEPPER POINT AND PADSTOW

*T*his *longer walk falls into three distinct and contrasting phases, making a varied, all-day expedition. The first section is along the dramatic cliffs from Trevone to Stepper Point. The cliff top is carpeted with wild flowers in summer and their scent can be quite heady on a hot, sunny day. But the spectacular cliff scenery reminds us what a wild place this is and the route passes two examples of an interesting geological phenomenon illustrating how this coast was, and is still being, shaped. After rounding Stepper Point the view becomes more pastoral and the path leads along the west side of the Camel estuary to the fishing port of Padstow. The final leg cuts across country and is easy walking on tiny lanes and good field paths. It makes a pleasing contrast to the earlier phases of the walk, partly because it is so quiet!*

Padstow has an enormous variety of places to eat including teashops, a famous fish restaurant and everything in between. But none has a view across the harbour and town to rival that of the tea gardens at Padstow Krazy Golf! It is a great place to sit (on a shady patio) and watch the world go by. They serve a selection of cakes, toasted teacakes and cream teas from the school half-term in February through to the October half-term. The hours are flexible; they serve as long as there are customers. Telephone: 07968 152796.

Light lunches and teas are also served at The Dower House and at Prideaux Place, passed a little farther on the walk. There is also a beach café at Trevone Bay.

DISTANCE: 7½ miles.

MAP: OS Explorer 106 Newquay and Padstow.

STARTING POINT: Trevone Bay car park (charge) (GR 891759).

HOW TO GET THERE: From the A389, Wadebridge Padstow road, a mile from Padstow take the B3276, signed 'Harlyn Bay 2¼ Trevone 1½'. Turn right, signed 'Trevone Bay' to either of two car parks at the end of the lane.

ALTERNATIVE STARTING POINT: If you wish to visit the teashop at the beginning or end of your walk, start in Padstow, where there are several signed car parks, which are very busy in the summer. The teashop is up the coast path from the north side of the harbour. You will then start the walk at point 6.

THE WALK

1. Facing the sea, take the cliff path to the right of the bay. The main path leads round the headland but it is worth diverting right to the Round Hole; then continue past it to rejoin the coast path. Continue for about two miles, passing Butter Hole. Be sure to stick close to the shore to see another, even more dramatic example of a geological phenomenon, Pepper Hole.

These 'holes' are an excellent illustration of how the forces of erosion have shaped the coast of Cornwall. A fault in the rock is gradually enlarged by the sea and forms a cave that gets bigger and bigger. Eventually the roof becomes unstable and part of it collapses, leaving a funnel-shaped hole connected to the sea by an arch. The erosion by the sea continues. Rain washes soil from the sides of the funnel and frost also helps shatter the rock until eventually the arch is also worn away, leaving a cove, as at Butter Hole.

2. After the tower, continue on the coast path as it swings round along the west side of the Camel estuary.

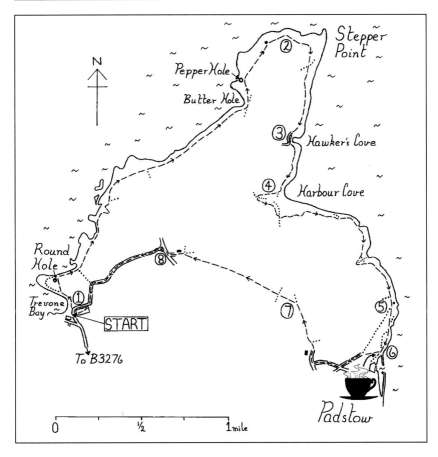

Stepper Point is 227 feet high and is crowned by the tower that acts as a landmark for mariners. The Camel is the only river of any size that comes out on the northern coast of Cornwall. This made it an important port and shipping harbour on the treacherous north Cornish coast. However, the sanctuary it offered was something of an illusion due to the perilous Doom Bar that stretches across the estuary, leaving a narrow deep-water channel below Stepper Point. Ships found themselves carried by unpredictable currents and winds onto the sand and over 300 of them have foundered, with great loss of life. Local legend says that the bar was formed by the curse of a mermaid mortally wounded by a fisherman who mistook her for a seal.

3. At Hawker's Cove the path joins a drive for a few yards before continuing down steps on the left. It shortly reaches a lane. Turn left for 50 yards then turn left to continue on the signed coast path.

4. At Harbour Cove follow the coast path as it cuts inland to steps down to a track. Cross the track and continue across a footbridge and ahead to a stile into a field. Over the stile turn left to a second stile on the left and press on to a T-junction with a track. Turn right for 30 yards then turn left to carry on along the waymarked coast path.

Alternatively, you can go down some steps to cut across the cove to pick up the track or, at low tide, walk further along the beach and rejoin the coast path at the end of the dunes.

5. Eventually, the path arrives at a war memorial above Padstow, a wonderful viewpoint across the Camel estuary. Take the left-hand fork down to the corner of the field and continue through a gate, for 30 yards to the teashop up some steps on the right.

Padstow's medieval network of narrow streets, which are decorated in the summer with window boxes of flowers, make it a pleasant place to explore. St Petroc came here (see Walk 4, page 26), founded a monastery and gave the town its name – Petroc's Stow. Despite the problems of the Doom Bar, Padstow retains a fishing fleet and harbour, backed by a wide quay and thronged with visitors in summer. Rick Stein, the chef who runs one of the best fish restaurants in the country and extols local fish on T.V., has boosted its fortunes in recent years. This has attracted several other gourmet restaurants. Always lively, Padstow is electric on May Day, when the Obby Oss comes to life. Opinions vary as to the origin of this romp – a fertility ritual, a rainmaker, a welcome to summer or a strategy to ward off the French! A large hooped mask, painted and plumed to represent a stylised horse, is danced madly through the streets from dawn to dusk, led on by a 'teaser' with a painted club and accompanied by dancers and musicians. It chases off men with its wooden snappers and tries to capture pretty girls beneath its capacious skirts. Those carrying the Oss change places regularly, usually outside the packed pubs, and a good time is had by all.

6. Turn left out of the teashop (turn right to explore Padstow) and return through the gate. Turn sharp left up the left-hand side of the field to a gate at the top. Go through the gate and walk along a road.

Trevone Bay

At a cross roads turn right then turn right again at a T-junction to pass in front of Prideaux Place. Go ahead under an arch and walk along the surfaced drive for almost a quarter of a mile.

St Petroc's original monastery is believed to have stood on the site of Prideaux Place. In AD 981 Padstow was sacked by the Vikings and the monks moved their main centre to Bodmin for safety. After the Reformation the land passed to the Prideaux family, who still own this fine Elizabethan mansion. During the Second World War the Army used it and some of the bedrooms are still as they left them. In recent years it has been used as a backdrop to many films and television programmes. It is open to the public on some summer afternoons. Telephone 01841 532411. One 17th-century Prideaux family member became a noted scholar and wrote 'Life of Mahomet'. The publisher to whom it was offered said that he wished there was more humour in it!

7. Turn left over a stile on a signed path across a field to a track. Cross the track and carry on in more or less the same direction from stile to stile to emerge at a farm. Turn left to a lane.

8. Turn right for 50 yards then turn left at a junction. This leads back to Trevone Bay and the start.

Walk 6
CRANTOCK AND PORTH JOKE

This interesting walk is hard to beat for diversity of landscapes – exposed, rocky headlands, wide, sandy surfing beaches, enormous dunes, a tidal estuary, fields and woodlands – are all visited in the few miles this route covers giving you a snapshot of Cornwall in miniature. Combine that with a village with a most picturesque core containing one of the National Trust's smallest properties, as well as an attractive tea garden, and you have all the ingredients of a most satisfying expedition.

The Cosy Nook Tea Garden in Crantock is a delightful, traditional establishment made most attractive by the many baskets full of flowers. There are some tables in the open, some protected by a pergola, and a few indoors. They serve a selection of cakes and other teatime goodies such as warm jam doughnuts, teacakes and, of course, cream teas. A tempting alternative is one of a wide choice of ice-cream sundaes. For lunch there are sandwiches, filled jacket potatoes as well as various platters – ploughman's with cheese, huntsman's with ham and fisherman's with mackerel. They are open every day between 11 am and 5 pm from Easter until mid October. Telephone 01637 830324. When the teashop is closed the pubs in Crantock serve food.

DISTANCE: 5 miles.

MAP: OS Explorer 104 Redruth and St Agnes.

STARTING POINT: Crantock Beach car park (National Trust, charge for non-members) (GR 789608).

HOW TO GET THERE: From the A3075, Newquay - Redruth road, a quarter of a mile south of its junction with the A392, take a minor road signed 'Crantock 1¾'. Turn right at a T-junction. Turn right, Halwyn Hill, signed 'Crantock Village and Beach' and follow the road through the village to the beach car park.

ALTERNATIVE STARTING POINT: There is very little parking in Crantock. If you wish to visit the teashop before the walk, park in the beach car park and walk back up the road into the village to the teashop on the left.

THE WALK

1. Return towards the car park entrance and take a path on the right, indicated by a green waymark. At the top of a steep rise bear left to stay behind the young dunes, heading just to the right of a house with very large picture windows. Level with the house, where there is a National Trust sign 'The Rushy Green' to the right, fork left then immediately right on a path looking out across sand dunes and Crantock beach on the right.

For more about sand dunes see Walk 8, page 43.

2. Go over a cross-path and ahead for 15 yards into a field. Bear right along the right-hand edge of the field then continue along the path on the cliffs at the western end of the bay. Carry on along the main coast path round the point into the next cove, Porth Joke, then along above the bay to eventually join a path coming in from the left down to the landward end of the bay and a footbridge across a stream.

Just after the deep cleft of Piper's Hole (see Walk 5, page 28 for more about 'holes' – and there is one on the headland further on) Pusey's steps lead down to the beach. They are named after Edward Pusey, an Oxford academic. When he fell foul of the university establishment in 1843, he was suspended for two years and came to stay near here. The steps are not difficult to negotiate. At low tide you can walk round to the first cave on the right. Just inside the entrance is a slab carved with a small horse, the outline of a woman and a few lines of verse:

> Mar not my face, but let me be
> Secure in this lone cavern by the sea
> Let the wild waves around me roar
> Kissing my lips for evermore.

The carvings are the work of a local man, Joseph Prater, and were completed in the early 1900s.

3. Cross the footbridge and turn left, inland. Walk up to and across a small car park to a track.

The name of this charming, unspoilt cove – Porth Joke – comes from 'chough', a distinctive, jackdaw-like bird with red legs and bill, which is now very rare. A local name for this cove is 'Polly Joke'. You may well see something unusual – cattle and sheep on the beach. The headlands, owned by the National Trust, are grazed and the animals sometimes come down onto the beach to drink from the stream and shelter from the wind. The grazing helps maintain the fine sward, full of wild flowers and at their beautiful best in early summer.

4. Turn left along the track. Press on uphill when it becomes a surfaced drive.

5. At a T-junction with a road turn right into Crantock. Just past Fairbank Hotel bear left. At a T-junction turn right to the teashop on the left.

Crantock gets its name from yet another of those Celtic saints that are so much a part of Cornwall's history – St Carantoc. His story is told in the modern stained glass of the church, not passed on this route. There is a holy well in the centre of the village, on the left just before the teashop, and in 1236 this remote community was chosen by the bishop to be a centre of learning. It has also been a centre of smuggling: the Old Albion Inn is reputed to have a secret hiding place beneath the floor. The centre of the village is charming and contains what must be one of the National Trust's smallest properties, donated to it in 1963.

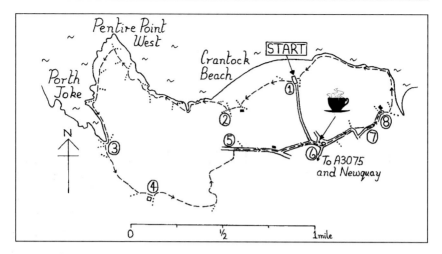

The Round Garden was probably the old village pound for holding stray animals but is now home to several ancient apple trees.

6. Return to the road and turn left, between the triangular village green and what appears to be a tree covered roundabout; in fact, the Round Garden. Cross the road and go ahead up Vosporth Hill. At the top of the hill, as the lane bends right, go ahead over a stile next to a field gate by a cross. Head across the field to another stile onto a lane.

7. Turn left.

8. Just after Penpol farm, at the end of a wall on the left, turn left through a gate and head down across a field to a small kissing gate. Follow the path through woods to a second kissing gate then ahead to walk on low cliffs above the estuary. When this eventually bends left, turn right down steps to the car park where this walk started.

The river on the right is The Gannel. Shipping used the mouth of the river until the 19th century. Cargo was off-loaded at Fern Pit, just before the car park, onto flat-bottomed riverboats to be taken on the flood tide three miles up-river to Trevemper. It was always a difficult passage along the channel next to the rocks on the opposite shore and ships were guided by 'hobblers' with ropes on the cliffs above. The traffic ceased due to silting up of the channel and the development of Newquay Harbour.

Walk 7
ST AGNES

*T*his *is an outstanding walk that encapsulates the essence of Cornwall. The outward leg combines fascinating industrial archaeology, made beautiful by setting and time, with dramatic cliff scenery as the path leads through heathland to Chapel Porth, a popular surfing beach backed by an excellent beach café. The heath is a blaze of colour in summer. Fortunately, the cliff path, though high, is fairly level. The return leg starts up a valley, once a hive of industrial activity but now a quiet haven filled with wild flowers, especially in spring. The climb continues to the top of St Agnes Beacon, over 600 feet above sea level, where your efforts are rewarded by views extending to 30 miles or more. It is therefore essential to choose a clear day to get the best from this energetic but rewarding route..*

 Chapel Porth is owned by the National Trust and has a very superior beach café. They offer a range of hot and cold sandwiches, the croque family being particularly delicious and sustaining. These are melted cheese sandwiches – monsieur (with ham), rosemary (mushrooms, cream and rosemary), fromage (sage and onion, my favourite) or de la mer (crab or prawns). On a cold day, the onion soup is very welcome. A selection of cakes, including delicious flapjack is also served. Or, on a hot day, the utterly sinful 'hedgehog' might tempt you – Cornish ice cream covered in clotted cream and rolled in honey-roast hazelnuts. This walk is energetic enough to justify anything! Unusually for a beach café, a range of teas is available as well as filter coffee. Most of the seating is outside, but there is some shelter. The opening hours are flexible, and depend on the weather and season but they are open every day from Easter until October and over Christmas and weekends for the rest of the winter. Telephone: 01872 552487.

There are also teashops, pubs and restaurants in St Agnes village.

DISTANCE: 6 miles.

MAP: OS Explorer 104 Redruth and St Agnes.

STARTING POINT: St Agnes village car park (GR 719504).

HOW TO GET THERE: From the A30 at its junction with the A390, take the B3277 to St Agnes. The car park is on Trelawney Road, on the left just before the clock.

ALTERNATIVE STARTING POINT: If you wish to visit the teashop at the beginning or end of your walk, start at Chapel Porth, where there is a large National Trust car park (charge for non-members). The teashop is at the rear of the car park. You will then start the walk at point 6.

THE WALK

1. Return to the main road and turn left through the village. Opposite the church bear left along Trevaunance Road.

As you walk along the main road on the left you pass St Agnes Miners' and Mechanics' Institute. Above the date, 1863, are the initials JPE, referring to John Passmore Edwards, a philanthropist who established many public buildings in Cornwall and other parts of the country. He was born nearby at Blackwater in 1823, the son of a carpenter and part-time publican, and became a successful newspaper proprietor.

2. Turn right on a track, Wheal Friendly Lane, signed 'Trevaunance Cove'. When the track finishes at a disused mine used as a theatre in the summer, press on along a path to a T-junction with another path. Turn left to a lane.

Look right for a view of Trevaunance Cove. Mining for tin, copper and other metals used to be very important in this area, as the numerous remains show, and the industry obviously needed a harbour. Several attempts to build one at Trevaunance Cove were made from 1632 onwards, but the sea always won in the end. The most successful was constructed in 1793 and lasted into the 20th century. Coal to drive the steam engines the mines depended upon was imported and ore exported. In 1915 a storm caused some minor damage that was not repaired and it wasn't long before the harbour had been reduced to a heap of stones.

3. Turn right for 30 yards then left, signed 'Polberro', on a path that starts along the drive to Little Orchard Cottage. Ignore a path on the right and carry on uphill to a T-junction with a track.

4. Turn right.

This part of Cornwall is formed from a huge intrusion of granite that pushed up from deep in the earth. Fluids associated with this were rich in metals, especially tin and copper, and formed veins that have been mined since prehistoric times. To begin with the metal was excavated from the surface and there are many overgrown trenches and pits. Flooding and the difficulty of raising the ore to the surface limited the depth to which the miners could work. These problems were solved by the introduction of steam driven pumps and winding gear in the early 19th century and most of the ruined mine buildings are associated with these. You may find this walk quite challenging, but think about the life the miners led. Some had to walk as much as nine miles to get to work then climb perhaps 500 feet down ladders before starting a long and arduous day's work in the cold and dark.

5. Immediately before a chimney turn right along a track. This leads to the coast path: turn left. Follow the path round Newdowns Head and St Agnes Head, forking right below the lookout. As the next mine buildings – Wheal Coates – come into view, fork right to stay on the coast path. This goes gently downhill to pass Towanporth Engine House. The left fork leads to the remaining buildings, where there is an information board giving more details. From the engine house follow the coast path to Chapel Porth and the teashop at the rear of the car park.

As you walk along the cliff path notice the metal frames. The dangerous mine

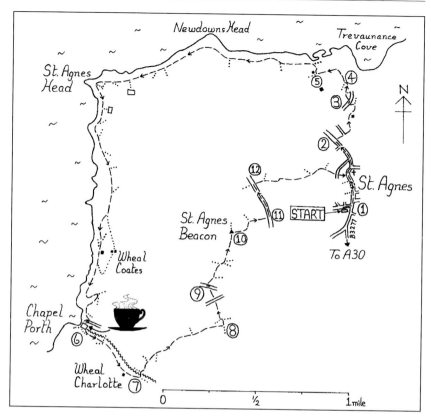

shafts used to be capped with concrete, thus entombing thousands of bats that roost in the subterranean workings during the day. Nowadays these metal frames are used so the public is protected but the bats can fly in and out.

6. Take a path over a footbridge at the rear of the café. When the waymarked coast path bends sharp right uphill, continue ahead up the valley, passing below Wheal Charlotte. Please note: this hillside is riddled with old shafts: you could lose dogs and children if they stray off the path.

This peaceful valley, filled with wild flowers, especially in spring, was once the scene of intense industrial activity. Powered by the fast-flowing stream, the tin ore from surrounding mines was processed here and some remnants of the works can still be found beneath the lush vegetation. Where the car park at Chapel Porth is today there used to be a stamping mill, where heavy crushers pulverised the rock into sand ready to separate the tin ore. This mill was driven by a 24-foot breast-fed water wheel and the lavatories are built into the remains of the wheel pit.

7. Some 150 yards after passing Wheal Charlotte turn left, shortly passing through a wooden kissing gate and crossing two streams, to a track. Turn right. When the track bends left, bear right, almost straight on, to continue up the valley to a stile by a gate onto a track.

8. Turn left along the track then left again at a T-junction after 50 yards. At the next T-junction, after a further 30 yards, turn right up to a lane. Cross the lane and continue in the same direction to a second lane.

9. Turn left for 25 yards then right along a track. Just before the track ends at a gate turn left on a path. Turn right at a T-junction and follow the path to the top of St Agnes Beacon.

The view from St Agnes Beacon is outstanding and there is a topograph to help you pick out the main features. It is said that you can see thirty church towers. Various uses have been made of this summit down the centuries. There are the remains of four Stone Age burial mounds and, as its name suggests, it has long been the site of a beacon. In the 18th century there was apparently a summerhouse here and in the Second World War there were gun emplacements, a radar station and Royal Observer Corps post.

10. From the top of the Beacon take a path on the right leading towards St Agnes village below and follow it down to a lane.

11. Turn left for 300 yards.

12. Turn right over a stile on a path signed 'To the village'. Walk along the left-hand side of a field. At the end of the field, cross a stile on the right and head diagonally across the next field to a stile onto an intermittently hedged path. This leads to a road on the outskirts of the village. Cross the road and carry on down a path between houses, to the centre of the village. (If you started at Chapel Porth, turn left here.) Turn right back to the start.

Walk 8
LELANT AND ST IVES

St Ives has something for everyone – a quaint old town full of charming nooks and crannies leading down to the harbour, a safe family beach, an exciting surfing beach and a rich artistic tradition. All these combine to make it the most attractive of honey pots and in the season it is swarming with people. Traffic is, thankfully, kept away from the centre and a park and ride scheme has been developed using the scenic branch line from St Erth. This allows us to park, walk and ride to explore this varied and interesting stretch of the Cornish coast, returning by train to the start.

In such a popular resort there is a profusion of refreshment stops. The Cortina Tea Garden is located just where this route enters St Ives. It prides itself on using proper leaf tea and also serves coffee or hot chocolate, welcome when the weather is less than clement, and it must be admitted that this can happen even in Cornwall! A choice of jams is available with a cream tea and they are happy to supply an extra plate if you wish to share. Another speciality is apricot and frangipane tart – a pastry case with frangipane topped with apricots and served with clotted cream. Other goodies include toasted teacakes and saffron cake. For a light lunch there is a choice of baguettes or ploughman's and soup. Most of the tables are in a courtyard, an ideal place to watch the world go by, and there is also some indoor accommodation. They are open between 10 am and 5.30 pm from May to September. Telephone: 01736 793353.

DISTANCE: 4 miles.

MAP: OS Explorer 102 Land's End

STARTING POINT: Lelant Saltings park and ride station car park. The car park is free. The fee quoted is for a return train ticket. You do not need this and should buy a single ticket from the conductor on the train for your return. It is wise to check the train times before you set off, as the route into St Ives does not pass the station (GR 543366).

HOW TO GET THERE: From the A30, Redruth-Penzance road, take the A3074 towards St Ives and follow the signs to the park and ride at Lelant Saltings.

ALTERNATIVE STARTING POINT: If you wish to visit the teashop at the beginning or end of your walk, start in the St Ives station car park (charge). The teashop is at the bottom of the steps at the entrance to the car park. You will then start the walk at point 7.

THE WALK

1. Return to the car park entrance kiosk and turn right through a gap in the hedge to a lane. Turn right along the lane for about a mile to a T-junction.

The lane passes Lelant station but the walk does not start here because most trains do not stop and the parking is much more limited.

Lelant was once an important port but lost out to St Ives when its anchorage became clogged with silt at the end of the Middle Ages.

2. Turn right. When the road bends left after 40 yards, continue ahead to the entrance to St Uny churchyard then take a path on the left signed 'Carbis Bay 2M'. Follow the path across a golf course and under the railway.

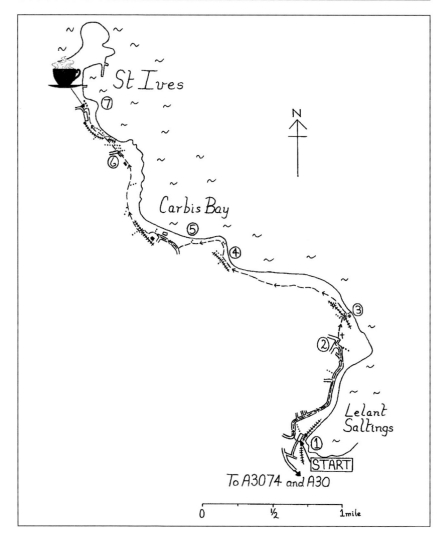

3. Immediately after passing under the railway, opposite a cottage, turn left on the coast path. Follow the main path behind the dunes and then, as the geology changes, along the cliffs through lush vegetation. After about a mile the path climbs up to meet the railway again.

Sand dunes begin life when wind-blown, dry sand collects behind an object on the beach such as driftwood or a stone. Pioneer plants such as marram grass

43

can colonize the pile and start the process of dune formation. This is an extremely harsh environment. The sand drains quickly so there is little water and what water there is tends to be salty. There is often drying wind and so, perverse as it seems, these plants are in most danger from dehydration. Not only that, they can often become covered by sand. Marram grass in particular has numerous adaptations to allow it to grow here. For example, the blades have a nifty arrangement whereby some cells act like hinges: when there is a shortage of water the blades curl up to limit their exposure to the wind whereas when there is plenty of water this hinge arrangement allows the blades to unfurl to absorb as much light and air as possible. The roots of the marram grass and other pioneer plants bind the sand and stop it blowing. When they die they add organic matter to the soil and allow it to hold more water. The dunes thus become suitable for other plants, which gradually supplant the marram grass. The dunes are now said to be fixed and support a wide variety of plants and hence insects, snails and so on. Since the sand contains a lot of shell fragments the soil formed is rich in calcium and many of the plants are those that are otherwise found on chalk. The dunes at this stage are sometimes called grey dunes because the sand has a darker tinge due to the organic matter that accumulates in it. They are still fragile and excess trampling will expose the sand, which soon starts blowing and puts the colonization process back to the start. The sand dunes here are a classic example of the ecological process known as succession which, left to itself, would result in woodland. However, this is interrupted by human activity; in this case, the golf course.

4. Some 15 yards after passing a crossing point over the railway, turn right, signed 'To Beach and Artist's Studio'. Continue along the path to Carbis Bay.

5. At Carbis Bay, a popular sandy beach, the path climbs up to a road. Turn right along the road as far as Carbis Bay Hotel then walk in front of the hotel. You can, if you wish, go down onto the beach instead and back up in front of the hotel. Carry on in the same direction along a path, up to and over the railway. Press on along the coast path, ignoring steps on the left to join a track coming in on the left.

The path passes a 'huer's' hut. This was a viewpoint from which a lookout would watch for shoals of pilchards in the bay. He would alert the crews of the fishing boats by crying 'Hevva' through a loudspeaker and then directing them towards their goal using semaphore-type signals made by oval bats called 'brushes'. *A local speciality was 'hevva cake', baked for the fishermen upon their return.*

☕ **6.** At a four-way junction continue ahead, downhill. When the path bends very sharp right, turn left on a smaller path to emerge at Porthminster beach. Bear left to walk behind a putting green to the teashop on the left.

Despite, or maybe even because of, the people that throng the town all season, St Ives is extraordinarily attractive. Its most notable physical feature is the headland called the Island. Apparently, it once really was separate. It divides the exposed surfing beach of Porthmeor from the harbour and safe bathing beach of Porthminster. At the topmost point is the small granite chapel of St Nicholas on the site of one built by St Ia, after whom St Ives is named. Yet another of the obscure Celtic saints, she came here from Ireland in the sixth century on an ivy leaf! This is probably a distorted memory of the fact that coracles were often lined with leaves.

Pilchards made St Ives prosperous and the houses had lower floors given over to salting and packing while the people lived upstairs. On catch days the streets apparently ran with fish oil and the stench was said to be indescribable; enough to stop the church clock, the local vicar once remarked! The area where the fishing families lived was called 'Downalong'. Higher up the town, in 'Upalong', the mining families lived. Relations between the two communities were not always cordial, with fights between groups of youths. Both faced disaster as the pilchard fishery failed (see Walk 15, page 72) and mining ended when the price of tin plummeted. Survival came from an unlikely source: the unique quality of the light and the appeal of the subject matter attracted an increasing number of artists and they were followed by tourists. So, fish cellars and net lofts were converted into studios and holiday accommodation. Numerous artists have made their home here and a branch of the Tate Gallery, overlooking Porthmeor beach, exhibits diverse examples, many inspired by this special environment. There is also the Barbara Hepworth Museum, dedicated to the work of perhaps the most notable of the artistic colony, the St Ives Society of Artists Gallery and many smaller, private galleries.

7. To explore St Ives turn left out of the teashop. Otherwise take some steps next to the teashop and turn left at the top to St Ives station and the train back to the start.

Walk 9
TREEN AND PORTHCURNO

*T*his *interesting walk is not very long or even very arduous, with just one short, sharp climb. None the less, it can easily take all day because there is so much to see en route. It is easy to spend an hour or two scrambling around Logan Rock. Next comes Porthcurno, a notable swimming and sunbathing beach. Just off the route in the village is a museum about Porthcurno's importance in telegraphic communications and the path goes directly past the famous Minack Theatre, open to visitors on the days when there is no matinee and incorporating an exhibition about its history. The return uses quiet field paths, passing an ancient church dedicated to one of those obscure Celtic saints. The coastal scenery is stunning and on the final approach to Treen there are some excellent views of inland Cornwall to enjoy.*

Porthcurno Beach Café is a very superior example of its kind with some tables outside. They offer an excellent range of home made cakes including meringues with clotted cream. Sinful – but delicious.

For lunch there are tempting baguettes including Brie and grapes or home made hummus with salad. An alternative is Cornish pasties baked on the premises. They are open from the week before Easter to the end of October from 'early until late'. Telephone: 01736 810834.

The coffee shop at the Minack Theatre is only open to those visiting the exhibition. There is no other source of refreshment on the route but there is a pub in Treen.

DISTANCE: 4½ miles.

MAP: OS Explorer 102 Land's End.

STARTING POINT: Treen village car park (charge) (GR 394229).

HOW TO GET THERE: From the A30 Penzance-Land's End road, take the B3283 through St Buryan, joining the B3315. Treen is signed on the left.

ALTERNATIVE STARTING POINT: If you wish to visit the teashop at the beginning or end of your walk, start in Porthcurno, where there is ample parking (charge). The teashop is across the road from the car park. You will then start the walk at point 4.

THE WALK

1. Return to the entrance to the car park and turn left for 15 yards then left again on a path signed 'Logan Rock' to shortly reach a track. Turn left for 100 yards. Go through a gate on the right and follow the path across four fields to the coast path.

To visit Logan Rock turn left along the coast path then bear right after 15 yards. To find the rocking stone needs quite a bit of scrambling over rocks and it is best reached by the path leading round to the right. After visiting the rock, return to the coast path and turn left along it.

There was an Iron Age fort here, Tretyn Dinas, and after 2,000 years the earthwork defences can still be made out. The distinctive, castellated headland behind is made of granite eroded into fantastic shapes. One of these is the famous Logan (pronounced loggan) rock. (See Walk 18, page 88) Weighing over 60 tonnes, it used to rock with a push from a finger. In 1824 a Lieutenant Goldsmith, nephew of the famous playwright and poet, came ashore with a group of sailors from their revenue cutter. For a bit of sport they dislodged the rock from its perch. There was a tremendous outcry, especially from the people of Treen, who then, as now, made a living from people coming to view the phenomenon. Lieutenant Goldsmith had to pay for it to be put back where it came from. It cost him £124.10s.6d (£124.52½ p), quite a sum in those days, but not, as is sometimes said, the ruin of him. Sadly, it was never quite the same and its fine balance was not restored.

2. If you do not wish to visit Logan Rock, turn right along the coast path. When the path shortly forks, take either branch: they join further on where a path leads back to Treen. At this point a path bears left. This also rejoins the coast path later. It has better views but goes up and down more.

☕ **3.** At a waymark post after a bare half mile turn left to stay on the coast path down to Porthcurno. Turn right along a track for 100 yards then turn left along a path signed 'Beach Café'.

Porthcurno is one of the best beaches in Cornwall. Much of the sand is fragments of seashells, which gives the sea its wonderful turquoise colour on a sunny day. But Porthcurno is famous for more than its beach. Since 1870 this cove has been the landing point for submarine cables linking Britain first to Bombay, then to Australia and the international telegraph network. Today it is fibre optic cables that come ashore. In 1934 the British Government pressed for a merger between the two most effective communications systems by combining Eastern Telegraph Company's cable services with the operating side of Marconi (see Walk 11, page 56) to create Cable and Wireless. Porthcurno became a major centre for research and development. Its work during World War II was so important that it was housed in a system of underground tunnels, complete with its own power station. The facility was closed in 1993 as modern developments had made it obsolete and the location of research and training moved elsewhere. The collection of equipment now forms the basis of a fascinating museum. This is open between 10am and 5pm every day except Saturday in the summer (though Saturdays as well in July and August). In winter it is open Sunday and Monday, closing at 4pm. Telephone: 01736 810966.

4. Return towards the beach and turn right to follow a path above the right hand side of the cove. Do not take the signed alternative path but continue for a few yards to some steps and climb these to the Minack Theatre.

Perched on the edge of the cliffs, and seeming to grow out of them, no theatre in the world can have a more inspirational setting. Its construction was the life's work of Rowena Cade, the daughter of a textile tycoon. She started in the

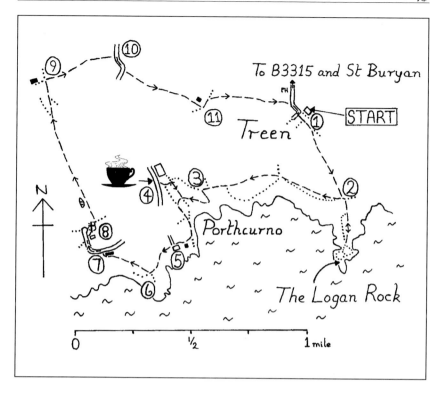

1920s *with the help of her gardener and based her design on a classical Greek amphitheatre. As the sun goes down behind the stage, this is a magical place. It opened in 1932 with a production of 'The Tempest'. The seating has been extended so it now holds 750 but performances are often sold out. Fog, wind and rain can add Cornish special effects but it is rare for a performance to be cancelled. How much better to be remembered for this remarkable achievement than as Lt Goldsmith, for an act of vandalism. The exhibition about the theatre is open throughout the year when there is no matinee.*

5. Cross the car park and carry on along the coast path.

6. As the path starts to descend to a rocky headland (and it is worth going as far as the headland for the view), turn right to walk with a wire fence on the right. Turn left in front of some houses to a lane.

7. Turn left and walk along the lane to a church on the right.

There has been a church here for about 1,500 years and it may well have been a religious site before then. St Levan was a sixth century member of the Cornish royal family and the name is a corruption of Seleven. The church has several interesting features, notably the carved bench ends, a tradition that has been maintained with some modern examples. As usual, there is more information within. Celtic saints had a penchant for striking things with their staff and St Levan was no exception. He split a rock in the churchyard and uttered the following prophecy:

When with panniers astride
A Pack Horse can ride
Through St Levan's stone
The world will be done.

Apparently the split has noticeably widened down the centuries. The stone may well have been the focus of pre-Christian fertility rituals.

8. Go into the churchyard and round to the back of the church to find a stone stile into a field at the top right-hand corner. Over the stile turn left. At the time of writing the path is not visible on the ground but goes in a more or less straight line from stile to stile across four fields. In the fifth field bear right to the top corner to find a track. Do not go along the track but cross a stile on the right. Head across a field to another stile a few yards to the left of a gate and continue to the top right-hand corner of the next field, level with the first farm building.

9. Turn right through a gate and follow the path from stile to stile across three fields to a lane.

10. Turn right for 100 yards then turn left on a signed path up the left-hand side of a field to a stile at the top. Head across the next field towards buildings to find a gateway and press on along the left-hand side of the next field.

11. At the end of this field turn left along a track for 65 yards then turn right into a field. Go to the far left-hand corner and follow the way-marked path, again from stile to stile, to Treen and the start.

Walk 10
LAMORNA AND THE MERRY MAIDENS

This superb walk explores one of the more challenging sections of the coast path in the Penwith peninsula. There are several short, sharp downs and ups and the path is rough in places, especially for the first half-mile or so. The reward is some wonderful coastal scenery and the chance to visit a tea garden that caters especially for walkers and which is on the coast path overlooking the sea at St Loy. The return starts up an almost sub-tropical wooded glen. This is followed by a stretch of road walking, made far more interesting by the chance to visit several of the early Bronze Age antiquities that have survived in this part of the world. After all that, it is a downhill stroll back to Lamorna.

Cove Cottage is perfectly positioned beside the coast path and serves teas and light lunches on a beautiful terrace overlooking a garden leading down to the sea. An amusing touch is the well-worn hiking boots used as planters. They serve a small selection of delicious cakes as well as cream teas and meringues. For a light lunch there is a choice of salads, using much of their homegrown, organic produce as well as filled baguettes. They are open every day except Monday from Easter until the end of September between noon and 6 pm. Telephone: 01736 810010.

When the teashop is closed the pub in Lamorna serves food.

DISTANCE: 5 miles.

MAP: OS Explorer 102 Land's End.

STARTING POINT: Lamorna Cove car park (charge) (GR 450241).

HOW TO GET THERE: From the B3315, Newlyn-Lands End road, take a minor road signed 'Lamorna Cove' to the car park on the quay.

ALTERNATIVE STARTING POINT: The tea garden is not accessible by road so there is no alternative start.

THE WALK

The cliffs here are made of granite, which has been extensively extracted, and the walk starts beside a disused quarry. The piles of rocks on the cliffs to the left of the bay are quarry waste. The harbour, itself constructed of granite, was used to export the rock, which was used to build many Victorian lighthouses and other structures, such as the Thames embankment.

1. Facing the sea, go to the right-hand side of the quay to pick up the coast path. When the track shortly ends the path leads up through rocks, as indicated by a not very obvious yellow waymark. Press on along the narrow path. At the top of some steps it is worth going left before continuing on the path. This is an excellent viewpoint and the rocks make a natural throne from which to enjoy it.

Derek Tangye was a debs' delight who came to Cornwall in 1950 with his wife Jeannie in search of the good life. He wrote about it in the 'Minack Chronicles', that being the name of the flower farm they bought. Watch for a gate on the right that gives access to Oliver's Land. In 1979 they bought 18 acres of land adjacent to their farm as a nature reserve, naming it after one of their cats. You can explore it, if you wish, and a board at the entrance gives more information.

2. Above Tater-du automatic lighthouse the path joins a track for a while. When the track turns right, inland, continue along the waymarked coast path.

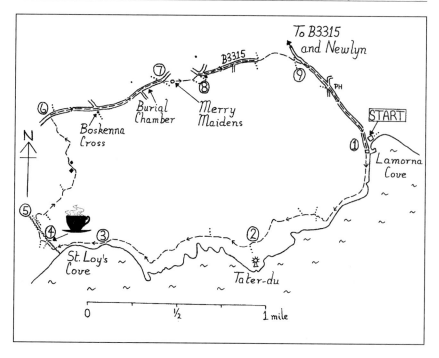

Tater-du lighthouse was installed in 1865 after a series of shipwrecks off this coast. The light can be seen for 16 miles and the foghorn is a complex of 72 speakers. None the less it did not prevent the Union Star from foundering in 1981, leading to the tragic loss of the eight-man crew of the Penlee lifeboat.

☕ **3.** The path eventually arrives at St Loy's Cove, where you have to pick your way across rounded boulders for about 50 yards. Follow the path into a wooded glen. At a cross-track turn right to the tea garden.

4. Return to the coast path and turn right. Follow the path up the glen to a stile onto a cross-path. Turn right, immediately crossing another stile, for 125 yards. Turn right, shown by a waymark on a post, to cross the stream. Continue by the stream for another 100 yards to a post signed 'To coast path'. Turn right here onto a track.

5. Turn left along the track and continue ahead when it joins another track coming in from the right. At a farm turn left to pass between the buildings of Boskenna Home Farm and continue to a road.

6. Turn right for half a mile.

The road passes Boskenna Cross, which at the time of writing has been removed for safe keeping following damage. Such prehistoric crosses are not Christian in origin, though they were sometimes later decorated with Christian symbols. They indicated a route for travellers in bygone days. This one originally stood in the middle of the road and was moved to protect it from damage by army lorries during World War II. A little further on, on the right of the road just after the entrance to Tregiffian Farm, is an early Bronze Age burial chamber. It was damaged during road works in 1840 and excavated in the 1960s. It contained a cup-marked stone with twelve oval and thirteen circular marks, which may refer to the number of full and new moons in a year. The original was taken to the County Museum in Truro. Cremated remains and an urn were also found.

7. Turn right, signed 'Footpath to Merry Maidens'. Having inspected the Maidens carry on across the field to a stile. Over the stile turn right to walk along the right-hand side of a field for 80 yards then turn left across the field to a stile back onto the road at a junction.

Properly called Boleigh Stone Circle, this ring of 19 standing stones is usually referred to as the Merry Maidens from the story that they are young girls turned into stone for dancing on a Sunday. In a nearby field are two, presumably related, upright stones called the Pipers, who were similarly petrified for providing the music. Other than the fact that the ring and associated stones date from around 2,400BC, nothing is known of their origin or significance, though they presumably had some ceremonial function.

8. Take a little lane to the left of a cottage. When the lane ends continue in the same direction on a signed bridleway and follow this to a road.

9. Turn right and follow the road through Lamorna back to the start.

Once only licensed to sell beer, the pub passed on the left is called 'The Wink' from the way customers used to ask the landlord for something stronger, and possibly contraband, from under the counter. Lamorna was popular with the Newlyn School of artists at the beginning of the 20th century, in particular S. J 'Lamorna' Birch, so-called to distinguish him from another member of the group called Birch.

Walk 11
MULLION AND POLURRIAN COVE

*T*his *excellent short walk starts at the ancient village of Mullion with its interesting 15th-century church before making its way out to the cliffs and to the site of one of the most significant events of the 20th century. It stays mainly at a high level with only one significant down and up at Polurrian Cove. There is some spectacular cliff scenery to enjoy before cutting back inland to tea at a craft centre and an easy stroll back to Mullion.*

The Coffee Shop at Mullion Meadows Craft Centre is most attractively situated in a complex of craft shops with tables in the courtyard round which they are clustered. They serve a selection of cakes and filled baps as well as cream teas and, on my visit, homemade waffles with maple syrup and Cornish ice cream. Delicious! They also make chocolates on the premises and a sample is served with tea. They are open every day between 10 am and 6 pm in summer and close just on Monday and Tuesday in winter. Telephone: 01326 241499.

There are also pubs and tea rooms in Mullion and the route passes two cliff-top hotels that serve refreshments to passers-by.

DISTANCE: 3½ miles.

MAP: OS Explorer 103 The Lizard.

STARTING POINT: Mullion village car park (GR 678193).

HOW TO GET THERE: From the A3083, Helston-Lizard road, about seven miles south of Helston take the B3296 to Mullion. Follow the signs round the one-way system to either of two car parks.

ALTERNATIVE STARTING POINT: If you wish to visit the teashop at the beginning or end of your walk, start at Mullion Meadows Craft Centre passed on the road to Mullion Cove where there is a large car park behind the complex of buildings. You will then start the walk at point 7.

THE WALK

Mullion is the largest village on the Lizard. The 15th-century church, dedicated to the Breton St Mellane, is worth a look for the carved bench ends, one showing Jonah inside the whale. Sheep dogs, attending with their masters, could leave by the 'dog door' in the studded south door when nature called.

1. Go into a small park across the road from the lower of the two car parks and follow the path across it to an exit on the far side. Turn right on a cross path that soon emerges on a road. Carry on in the same direction to a T-junction. Cross the road to continue in the same direction on a path that leads through to a lane and press on along the lane in the same direction.

2. At a post box on the left turn sharp right, almost back on yourself, signed 'Stable Cottage'. Turn left behind a gate and follow the waymarked path across a field, through a narrow belt of trees and across a second field to a small wooden gate giving on to a track.

3. Turn left for about half a mile. At the second right-hand bend turn left through a gate to continue in the same direction on a signed path across a field to the Marconi Monument on the cliff edge.

In 1900 Marconi shocked his board of directors by asking for £50,000 to investigate sending wireless signals across the Atlantic. Everyone else at that time thought that such over the horizon communication was impossible and the

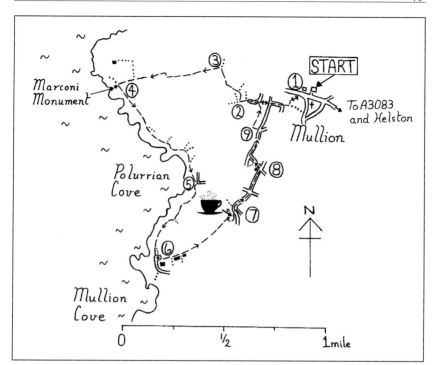

furthest that a signal had been sent at that date was less than a hundred miles. Despite this, Marconi had faith in his dream and selected Poldhu as the site of his 'great experiment'. Work began in October 1900 and was on a huge scale compared with what had gone before. It was fraught with difficulties due to bad weather but on 12th December 1901 the team successfully sent the three dots of the letter 'S' to Newfoundland and so ushered in the modern era of global communications. 'Unmistakeably, the three sharp, little clicks corresponding to three dots sounded in my ear,' *Marconi later wrote,* ' but I would not be satisfied. "Can you hear anything, Mr Kemp?" I said. . .'. *This was the start of many landmark achievements of Poldhu station, which was at the forefront of the development of long distance radio communication. Its work came to an end in 1934 and Marconi's daughter unveiled the Marconi Monument when the field was cleared in 1937. The centenary of the first transatlantic signal was celebrated by the opening of the Marconi Centre in the small building to the right of the field. It is open on Sunday afternoons and sometimes in the summer.*

4. Turn left along the coast path. When the path forks, bear right to stay on the coast path down to Polurrian Cove and up the steps on the other side to join a path. Turn right up to a road.

5. Turn right immediately along a track* and when the track ends, continue in the same direction to a turning circle just before Mullion Cove Hotel. It is worth going to the far end of the hotel for the best views of the Cove but do not continue down to it unless you want to climb back up.

Soon after you start along the track look for part of a wall on the right, seaward, side. This is all that remains of two houses that once stood here and have succumbed to erosion of the cliffs. Ninety years ago the coast path was on the other side of those houses.

Mullion Cove is protected from winter gales by two stout sea walls. They were completed in 1895 by Lord Robartes of Lanhydrock (see Walk 16, page 79) as recompense to the local fishermen for several disastrous pilchard seasons. The Cove had a lifeboat station from 1867 until 1909, and with good reason: in the six years up to 1873 there were nine wrecks along the mile and a half of coast under Mullion cliffs.

6. From the turning circle take a signed path leading inland. This shortly leads to a track behind some houses. Continue in the same direction for 65 yards. When the track bends sharp right continue ahead to the left of a house to a stile into a field. Walk along the right-hand side of the first field and the left-hand side of a second to a gate to the right of a farm building. Follow the track down to a road and Mullion Meadows Craft Centre.

7. From the Craft Centre turn left along the road.

8. Take the second road on the left, immediately after the Ridgeback Lodge Hotel. At a T-junction turn right along Laflouder Fields.

9. Immediately after number 10, at a bus stop, turn left on a signed path and follow this to a T-junction with a lane. Turn right and immediately right again on a path to retrace your steps back to the start. (If you started at Mullion Meadows, turn left here to pick up the route at the end of point 1 – but then you miss out on exploring Mullion.)

Walk 12
KYNANCE COVE AND THE LIZARD

This outstanding walk is one of the 'must do's' of Cornwall. The route visits the most southerly point of mainland Britain, the scenery is spectacular and the natural history is fascinating. I do think it needs a sunny day to enjoy it at its wonderful best. This is one of the most magical places in England when the sun is shining, the sea is turquoise and the heather is in bloom.

The Honeysuckle Tea Rooms have been meeting the needs of visitors for about 50 years but the building is far older than that. It is said to date in parts from the 14th century and has at least two ghosts! A good selection of cakes is served along with other teatime goodies including Cornish saffron buns, teacakes and shortbread. For lunch the choice ranges from sandwiches, filled jacket potatoes through a wide selection of pasta dishes to full meals including daily specials. The Honeysuckle is open from 10.30 am to the evening from Easter to October and occasional winter weekends if the weather is good. Telephone: 01326 290662.

You will not be short of opportunities for refreshment on this walk. An alternative choice, earlier on the route, is the Wave Crest café near the most southerly point. There is also a good beach café at Kynance Cove and the Housel Bay Hotel, which has a delightful terrace overlooking the sea, serves refreshments to walkers on the coast path.

DISTANCE: 5 miles.

MAP: OS Explorer 103 The Lizard.

STARTING POINT: Kynance car park (National Trust, charge for non-members) (GR 688132).

HOW TO GET THERE: From the A3083, Helston-Lizard road, about half a mile north of Lizard village, take a signed road to the car park.

ALTERNATIVE STARTING POINT: If you wish to visit the teashop at the beginning or end of your walk, start in Lizard village, where there is parking on the village green. You will then start the walk at point 5.

THE WALK

1. In the field part of the car park find a gap in the wall signed 'View point only'. Follow the path to the viewpoint overlooking Kynance Cove. If you wish to go down to the cove – and it is well worth it – the path leads from the far end of the car park and you have to return to the car park to start the walk.

A vision of white sand, turquoise water, islands, stacks and arches, Kynance must be one of Cornwall's most beautiful places. The name is derived from the Cornish 'kewnans', meaning ravine. Giant mounds of multicoloured serpentine rise through the sand. One was called Albert Rock after Prince Albert brought his children here in 1846. The golden cap the outcrops wear is not part of the rock; it is a lichen called Xanthoria. To the west of the cove and among the islands are interconnected caves that you can explore at low tide; they have splendid Victorian names such as the Ladies' Bathing Pool and the Drawing Room. When the conditions are right there are also spectacular blowholes.

2. Turn left along the cliffs to eventually join the main coast path leading from the car park. Turn right along it for nearly three miles, passing Old Lizard Head, Lizard lighthouse and Housel Bay Hotel.

As you start walking from Kynance to Lizard, the land beside the path is not cultivated. This is not for conservation reasons but because the soil produced by the weathering of serpentine is not very fertile but rich in magnesium. It

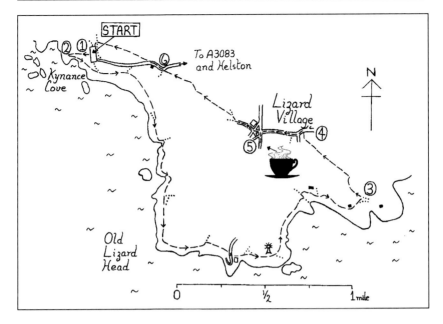

supports a distinctive community of wild flowers that produce a blaze of colour in the spring and summer. Soon this gives way to cultivated land beside the path. This indicates a change in the underlying geology, from serpentine to mica schist, which weathers into a much more fertile soil. Schists are an example of metamorphic rock; that is, rock that has been altered by exposure to heat and pressure. The mica schist was produced from the sediments on the ocean floor when they were 'cooked' by the heat and pressure of the serpentine. Further on still, as you round the point, the rocks change again to hornblende schist, produced from lava.

On a calm summer's day it is difficult to imagine just how dangerous this coast can be but many ships have come to grief, dashed on the rocks offshore. The first lighthouse was built here in 1619. New technology was introduced in 1752, when the lights came from coal fires, kept bright with bellows. Apparently one passing ship noticed that the lights were dim and so the captain ordered a shot to be fired to alert the keepers. The gunners were a bit too enthusiastic and their shot breached the walls of the lighthouse.

If you wish to cut the walk short, there are several signed paths that lead to Lizard village. Pick up the route again at point 5.

3. When the coast path bears right towards a white tower, Lloyds Signal Station, bear left to a gate onto a track. Turn left along the track.

A firm of shipping agents in Falmouth built the original signal station in 1872 so company agents could semaphore passing ships and relay news of cargoes to London. The present building dates from 1954 and is now a private residence. To the left of the path is a building used by Marconi in his pioneering work on radio communications (see Walk 11, page 56). It is open to the public on some summer afternoons.

☕ **4.** At a T-junction with a road turn left and walk into Lizard village. At a crossroads in the middle of the village turn left to the teashop on the left.

Serpentine comes in a variety of colours depending on its exact mineral composition but all the forms are easy to work and polish up beautifully. There are many shops selling ornaments and jewellery in the village. When Queen Victoria was here in 1846 she ordered a serpentine table and it became very fashionable. It was even used as a building material, but this didn't last long because it is damaged by the somewhat acid rain in urban areas.

5. Turn right out of the teashop and return to the village centre. Turn left, signed 'Coastal Path' to walk with the green, sadly covered with cars in the summer, on your right. At the end of the green continue ahead for 100 yards then bear right on a track, signed 'Public footpath to Kynance Cove'. After 50 yards do not go through a field gate but bear left up some stone steps to continue on a raised path. Follow the path, no longer raised, down into a dip and up the other side to eventually reach the access road to the car park.

This raised path is on top of the boundary between two fields, an unusual catwalk that is an ancient thoroughfare, used by farmers to get to their outlying fields. There are excellent views and one striking feature is how flat the Lizard is inland. This stable, level platform makes it an excellent site for the Goonhilly satellite communications station, whose giant dishes dominate the landscape.

6. Turn left along the access road to just past a house called 'Carn Goon'. Take a path bearing right. This leads across the heath to the bottom of the car park where this walk started.

Walk 13
HELFORD AND MANACCAN

This charming and interesting walk explores the unspoilt countryside round the Helford river, including Frenchman's Creek, made famous by Daphne du Maurier in her novel of the same name. The route also visits two appealing and very different villages. The Helford river is most attractive scenically when the tide is in. Its biological importance is more obvious when the tide is out and many species of birds work the mud revealed to find their food.

 The Sunflower Tea Rooms at Myrtle Nursery on the edge of Manaccan offers a friendly and personal welcome as well as delicious home made cakes and scones and a reviving cup of tea. It is perched on the edge of a steep slope and has an outstanding view from the window. It is open between 10 am and 5 pm every day except Tuesday and Wednesday from Easter until the beginning of October. Telephone: 01326 231604.

When the tea room is closed, pubs in both Manaccan and Helford serve food. There is also a tea room, Rose Cottage, in Helford, again only open in the summer months, very well positioned over looking the creek. This serves a good selection of sandwiches as well as cream teas.

DISTANCE: 5 miles.

MAP: OS Explorer 103 The Lizard.

STARTING POINT: Helford car park (GR 759261).

HOW TO GET THERE: From the B3293, Helston-St Keverne road, five miles south of Helston, take a minor road east signed 'St Martin 2¼, Manaccan 4 Helford 5'. Go through Newtown and follow the signs to Helford. The car park (charge) is on the right, before the village.

ALTERNATIVE STARTING POINT: If you wish to visit the teashop at the beginning or end of your walk, there is a parking area next to Manaccan Methodist chapel near Myrtle Nursery. The Methodist church is outside the village and is passed on the way to Helford about a mile and a half from Newtown. You will then start the walk at point 8.

THE WALK

1. Return to the road and turn right into Helford. Turn right over the creek then right again to walk alongside the creek as far as the Shipwright's Arms.

2. Go through the pub car park then turn left along a cross track, signed as a footpath, for 100 yards and then turn right to stay on the signed path. Follow the path down to Penarvon Cove and then follow an initially surfaced track up through woodland. Continue ahead as a surfaced track joins from the right.

One species whose existence has not been confirmed scientifically is Morgawr, the legendary Helford monster. First sighted in 1926, he is described as a hideous, hump-backed creature with stumpy horns!

3. At a T-junction turn right along a track, signed 'Frenchman's Creek'. When the track forks take the left, smaller branch downhill.

4. At the bottom of the hill do not go through a gate across the track but turn left down a few steps and through a wooden kissing gate to walk beside Frenchman's Creek, shortly passing a welcome seat

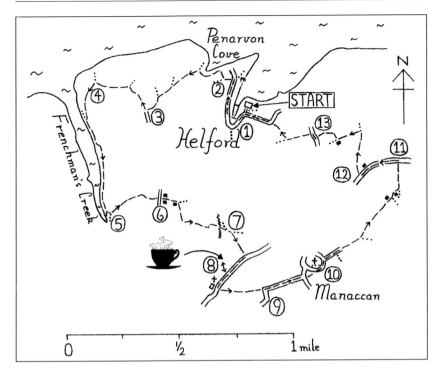

well-placed to admire the view. When the path appears to fork, bear left uphill (the right branch just leads to the creek) for 50 yards to a T-junction with a track.

Frenchman's Creek was immortalised by Daphne du Maurier's (see Walk 17, page 81) 1941 novel of the same name, where the heroine, Dona St Colomb, met her pirate lover. All highly romantic stuff!

5. Turn left and follow the track up to a lane.

6. Cross the lane and follow the path between farm buildings. Some 20 yards after the last building go through the right-hand gate of two and walk down the right-hand side of a field. At the bottom go through a gate and turn left. Walk along the edge of a field as far as a stile on the left. Cross the stile into woodland and follow a path round to the right to find some steps down to a stream. Cross the stream and continue ahead, joining a path coming in from the left.

☕ **7.** Some 20 yards after the junction turn right through a small metal gate into a field and walk up the right-hand side of the field to a lane. Turn right for 100 yards then right along a track to Myrtle Nursery. The tea room lies beyond the nursery.

8. Return to the lane and turn right past the Methodist chapel to a signed path on the left. Follow this from stile to stile across three fields to a lane, bearing half left in the first field, straight across the second and along the right-hand side of the third.

9. Turn left along the lane into Manaccan. At a T-junction go straight ahead on a path in front of some cottages to the Post Office and turn right.

This most attractive village is first mentioned in a charter of AD967. The church has a 200-year-old fig tree growing out of the southeast wall. In 1791 William Gregor found the mineral manaccanite near the village, from which the metal titanium was first extracted.

10. Turn right again, signed as a footpath, opposite gates into the churchyard. When the main path bends right, continue ahead on a signed path over a stone stile beside a field gate. Follow the path to a farm. Bear to the left of barns to pick up a surfaced drive and walk along this to a T-junction with a lane.

11. Turn left.

12. Some 80 yards after a thatched cottage on the right turn right on a signed path and follow it along the right-hand side of two fields to a track. Turn left, signed 'To Helford'. Opposite the first farm building turn right along the right-hand side of a field for 50 yards then turn left across the field to a stile onto a lane.

13. Turn right for 50 yards then left on a signed path along a surfaced drive. At the end of the first field turn right off the drive and walk down beside a hedge on the left to a lane. Turn left back to the car park where this walk started.

Walk 14
FLUSHING AND MYLOR

*T*he area around the river Fal is one of the prettiest in Cornwall but it is not easy to explore on foot, as there are many parts with few paths. This walk is one exception. It starts at one attractive village, facing across the river to Falmouth, and climbs over the hill to the next creek and the village of Mylor. This is an ancient community with a long maritime tradition, today represented by a busy marina. The return is an easy stroll round a headland with extensive views across the river to the attractive countryside beyond.

Mylor Harbour Café has a pleasant interior in keeping with its setting and also some tables outside overlooking the marina. The menu is designed to meet the hearty appetites of sailors and includes breakfast. They serve a tempting selection of cakes and desserts, including raspberry or rhubarb frangipane with cream, and, of course, cream teas. Possibilities for lunch range from sandwiches through soup and salads to full meals such as moules marinière. There is a choice of teas or in winter you might be tempted by hot chocolate with whipped cream and marshmallow. They are open from 8 am every day throughout the year. Telephone: 01326 373712.

DISTANCE: 4 miles.

MAP: OS Explorer 104 Redruth and St Agnes or 105 Falmouth and Mevagissey.

STARTING POINT: Flushing Quay (charge) (GR 808337).

HOW TO GET THERE: From the A39, Truro-Falmouth road, follow the signs to Flushing, passing through Mylor Bridge. In Flushing turn right past the War Memorial at a phone box onto the quay. If this car park is full or you think you might return after 6 pm, continue along the road through the village, past Flushing Sailing Club, where there is some roadside parking. Walk back to the quay to start the walk. Alternatively, park in Falmouth and get the ferry to Flushing (Telephone: 07974 799773).

ALTERNATIVE STARTING POINT: If you wish to visit the teashop at the beginning or end of your walk, start in Mylor, where there is a car park (charge) just past the teashop. You will then start the walk at point 7.

THE WALK

If you are worried about the weather, have a look at the barometer on the wall of the end house facing the quay. Flushing is said to have the mildest climate in England. This community was originally called Nankersey. The Trefusis family, landowners round here since before the Norman Conquest, decided to develop a harbour to rival Falmouth. They brought over Dutch engineers from Vlissingen and the corruption of that became Flushing. The Dutch influence can still be seen in some of the older buildings.

1. With your back to the quay turn left past the War Memorial then left along the road. Take the second road on the right, Kersey Road, by the Royal Standard pub.

2. Opposite Kersey Close turn left on a path signed 'Mylor Church'. Cross a stile and continue up the left-hand side of a field to a stile on the left at the end of the field. Over the stile, go ahead a few yards to a stile by a gate giving onto a surfaced drive.

3. Turn left. At a road junction continue ahead for 70 yards.

4. Turn right on a footpath signed 'Trelew'. The path starts along the

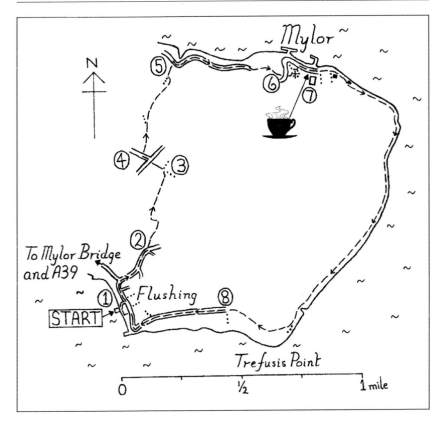

left-hand side of a field then continues ahead when the hedge turns left. Follow the path down through woods, ignoring a path bearing left, to a T-junction with a track. Turn right to a lane.

5. Turn right. This very quiet lane is made even better for walking by a raised path on the right. When the lane becomes a path, press on to a road.

6. Cross the road and go through the churchyard to emerge at Mylor Marina and the teashop on the right.

There has been a church here since the early fifth century. It was initially established by St Mylor, who came as a missionary from Brittany and set up a monastery here. To complicate matters there is a second St Mylor, of a later and uncertain date. He was the son of the king of Cornwall. His father died before he came of age and his uncle became regent. When young Mylor converted to Christianity, his uncle did not approve and cut off bits of his anatomy to try to persuade him to change his mind. When this did not work, his uncle finished matters by chopping off Mylor's head. It is believed that the young martyr was buried in the churchyard. Some of the existing gravestones will raise a smile. Look for that of Joseph Grapp near the east window and of Thomas James, smuggler, near a fork in the path. The churchyard also contains the Ganges Memorial to the boys who died while training for a career in the Navy. The church has several interesting features and there is more information available within.

Looking at the peaceful scene at Mylor today it is hard to believe its busy history. It was once Royal Dockyards where the packet ships that delivered mail worldwide were repaired and victualled. It was also used by French resistance fighters and American troops during World War II.

7. Turn right out of the teashop. Continue by the estuary, as the road becomes a track then, after the entrance to Penarrow House, a path. At Restronguet Sailing Club the path crosses the slip then goes up steps and to the right of a small building. Follow the path round the headland and continue ahead when it becomes a track after a gate.

Trefusis Point was originally chosen by Henry VIII as one of four sites for castles to defend the ports in the river Fal. In the end it was decided that two were sufficient and the planned castle was never built. One of the two that were constructed, Pendennis Castle, can be seen ahead, above Falmouth.

8. Go through a second gate and carry on along the road into Flushing. At Flushing Sailing Club follow the road round to the right. Turn left down a short, cobbled passageway to the quay.

Walk 15
MEVAGISSEY AND HELIGAN GARDENS

This walk is longer than most in this book as well as being one of the most energetic, especially near the start; ideal if you have over-indulged in cream teas and need to burn off some calories! The walk starts with an exhilarating section of coast path. This stretch has dramatic cliff scenery – and several sharp climbs and descents. This exertion is followed by a delightful level stretch along the Pentewan valley before another climb to Heligan and the famous gardens. Sadly, the gardens generate a lot of traffic and what should be a quiet lane can be uncomfortably busy, but there is no other route. A brisk ten-minute march and you are there. It takes several hours to see the gardens properly so to combine a visit with this walk would make for a very long day. Suitably refreshed, you will find the last part of the walk sheer delight as an easy track leads down a wooded valley back to the start with many pleasing views over this landscape of rounded hills and deep coombes.

The busy Willows Restaurant at Heligan Gardens has a vine growing around it. There are some tables outside. They serve cakes, cream teas with delicious scones and excellent shortbread. The Servery offers filled jacket potatoes, sandwiches, salads and a choice of hot meals using fresh produce from the garden, between noon and 2.30 pm. They are open 10 am until 6 pm in summer and close at 5 pm in winter. Telephone: 01726 845100.

There are also several tearooms and restaurants in Mevagissey.

DISTANCE: 7 miles.

MAP: OS Explorer 105 Falmouth and Mevagissey.

STARTING POINT: Mevagissey harbour (GR 015448).

HOW TO GET THERE: Mevagissey is reached along the B3273 from the A390 at St Austell. Park in any of the signed car parks and make your way through the narrow streets to the landward side of the harbour.

ALTERNATIVE STARTING POINT: If you wish to visit the teashop at the beginning or end of your walk, start at Heligan Gardens, where there is ample parking. The teashop is at the entrance to the gardens. You will then start the walk at point 7.

THE WALK

History's first mention of Mevagissey is in 1313 and the name comes from two Irish missionaries, Meva and Itha. Once famous for fast ships and pilchards, the fishing industry was at its height in the 19th century. Thousands of tons were landed here for salting, packing and export to southern Europe and the Royal Navy, who called them Mevagissey ducks. Towards the end of the 19th century the pilchards deserted Cornish waters for reasons that are not entirely clear – a combination of over-fishing, pollution and climate change perhaps – and though there are fishing boats in the attractive harbour and lobster pots on the quay, the main business today is tourism.

1. Facing the sea, walk along the left side of the harbour for a few yards then bear left uphill on a path signed 'To the Coast Path'. Follow this up past cottages and then up some steps into a recreation ground. Cross this to find the coast path just to the right of the last house.

2. Follow the coast path. Immediately after crossing a footbridge, bear left: the right branch leads down to the beach. The path hugs the clifftop along the right-hand side of several fields and eventually leads across a second footbridge. A path leads straight ahead up the field while the right of way coast path leads round the field to the right. Both lead up to a double stile giving onto a path above a road.

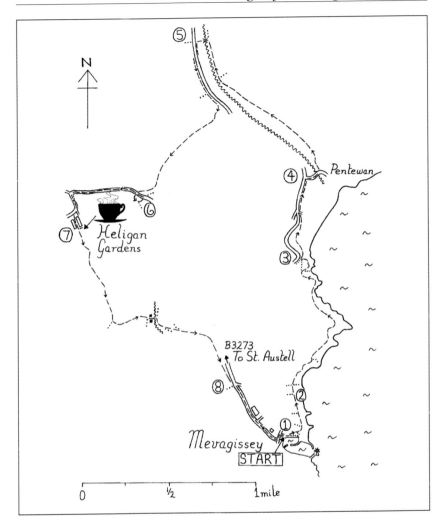

3. Turn right and follow the path until it emerges on the road at the entrance to a caravan site. Continue in the same direction along the road to a junction.

Pentewan, pronounced Pen-tuan, is a former quarrying village and local Pentewan stone was used in many Cornish buildings such as Restormel Castle (see Walk 16, page 78). A port was created in 1826, which exported stone and china clay until the end of the First World War.

73

4. Turn right, signed 'Pentewan'. Immediately over a bridge turn left, signed 'Pentewan Valley Trail'. Follow the track for about three quarters of a mile to a riverbank and then bear right up river as far as a bridge. Cross the bridge and follow the track ahead to the main road.

5. Turn left then cross the road to continue in the same direction, following the cycleway signs. Continue as the track first runs parallel with the road and then turns right to climb through woods. Follow it under a bridge and then left round to a lane.

6. Turn left. Continue round a left-hand corner, passing a road on the right, to the entrance to Heligan Gardens. Turn left on a signed footpath along a track to the right of the entrance. Turn left at a pedestrian crossing to the tearoom at the garden entrance.

The Tremayne family acquired the estate in the 16th century and it remained in their hands until 1970. Down the years succeeding generations nurtured a complex of farmland, woods, the earliest brickworks in Cornwall and, of course, gardens. The First World War took most of the gardeners away from the estate and the house was requisitioned as a military hospital. Then, in 1943, American forces used Pentewan beach as a training ground for the Normandy landings and the officers were billeted here. Slowly the gardens became lost under a confused jungle of ivy and brambles. Largely at the instigation of Tim Smit of Eden Project fame, the garden has been rescued and brought back to its Victorian prime, a process recorded by television cameras in a brilliant publicity coup. There is a lot to see including an immaculate walled kitchen garden with adjacent orangeries housing passion fruit, bananas and manure-heated pineapple pits. The word Heligan is from the Cornish for willows, hence the name of the restaurant. The garden is open every day and a visit is likely to take at least a couple of hours.

7. Return to the track and turn left. At a metal gate across the track turn left and follow the track down to a few houses. Cross a footbridge and turn right. Walk along the track: the parallel path accessed by a stile on the right is not a right of way. When a track joins on the left, continue ahead to a road.

8. Turn right, back to Mevagissey.

Walk 16
LOSTWITHIEL

*T*he *Fowey Valley above Lostwithiel is a lovely corner of Cornwall, as the rich and influential have recognised down the centuries. This walk is a one-way route down the valley from the Lanhydrock estate to the ancient stannary town of Lostwithiel, once the capital of Cornwall. The walk is perhaps the easiest in this book as it is mainly on the level or downhill and much of the route is on surfaced drives and tracks. The train does the hard work of getting back up the valley to the start and it was the view from this stretch of line that was the germ of the idea for this walk. An easy half-mile stroll returns you from the station to the start.*

Muffins is housed in one of Lostwithiel's attractive old houses on Fore Street. The building dates from the late 18th century and one of the first inhabitants was Captain George Lawrence, who had sailed with Captain Bligh of *Bounty* fame. He ran a Naval Training School in the building, died in 1846 and his ghost is said to haunt the building. As well as the charming interior there is a pleasant garden at the rear beneath the spire of the town's ancient church. Muffins specialises in the best of Cornish produce and their ploughman's lunch, for example, features Yarg cheese. They serve a small selection of delicious homemade cakes. As well as cream teas, a gentleman's tea is offered consisting of a cheese scone and cake. They are open between 10 am and 4.30 pm Monday to Saturday and on Sundays during high season. Telephone: 01208 872278.

When the teashop is closed on Sundays in winter, there are several pubs in Lostwithiel that serve food.

DISTANCE: 4½ miles.

MAP: OS Explorer 107 St Austell and Liskeard.

STARTING POINT: Respryn Bridge car park. (GR 099635).

HOW TO GET THERE: From the A30 at Bodmin take the A38 towards Liskeard for a few hundred yards. Turn right, signed 'Lostwithiel', for half a mile then turn left, signed 'Respryn 1', to a car park on the left just before a bridge.

ALTERNATIVE STARTING POINT: If you wish to visit the teashop at the beginning or end of your walk, start in Lostwithiel, where there is a car park signed from the A390. Leave the car park using the pedestrian access and ahead across one street to a second. Turn left. You will then start the walk at point 5. There is also parking at Bodmin Parkway station if it is more convenient to start there (point 6). You can reach Bodmin Parkway by steam train from Bodmin. Telephone: 01208 73666.

TRAIN INFORMATION: Please check train times before you start as trains from Lostwithiel to Bodmin Parkway are not frequent, especially on a Sunday. Telephone: 08457 484950.

The Walk

1. Return towards the entrance to the car park and take a path on the left that shortly leads back to the road just before the bridge over the river Fowey. Turn left over the bridge then right through a gate. Turn right down a couple of steps to walk beside the river to a footbridge. Cross over and carry on along the right-hand bank of the river. Continue in the same direction when the river bends left. Go through a gate across the path and ahead for 35 yards.

2. Turn left and shortly go through a gate bearing a sign 'Footpath to Restormel Castle'. Follow the path up to a gate and across a field to a gate onto a track. Walk along the track, which shortly becomes a surfaced drive to water works passed on the left. When the main drive

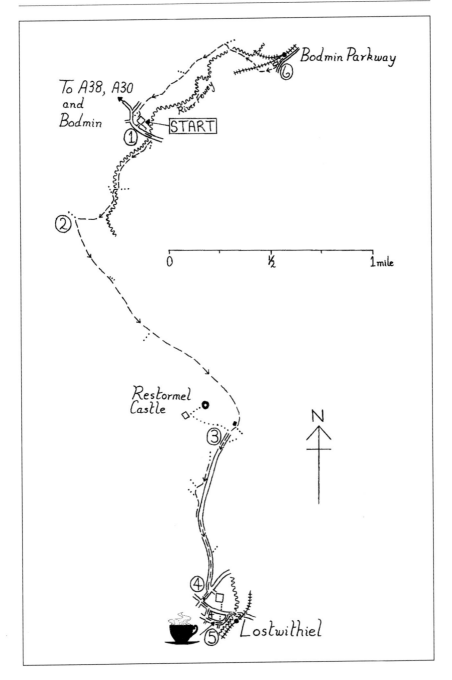

To A38, A30
and
Bodmin

START

① ② ③ ④ ⑤ ⑥

River Fowey

Bodmin Parkway

Restormel
Castle

Lostwithiel

N

0 ½ 1 mile

bends right, press on ahead to eventually arrive at a farm. Continue between farm buildings to a gate.

To visit Restormel Castle (charge) turn right up a drive to a car park then turn right through a gate into the castle grounds. This is the only uphill part of the walk but is well worth the effort involved. The castle, in the care of English Heritage, is open daily from April to October.

Restormel Castle stands on a hill commanding the important river crossing at Lostwithiel and the views from the ramparts are magnificent. The walls of the keep are 30 feet high in places and it is surrounded by a dry moat, lined with flowers in spring. The excellent guide and informative plaques help bring the ruin to life.

3. Carry on along what is now, according to the map, a lane rather than a drive but is not much different!

By a seat on the right there is a pedestrian access onto a path parallel with the lane that rejoins it further on. This is not a right of way but seems to have been made so pedestrians do not have to walk all the way along the lane.

☕ **4.** At a main road turn right along the pavement for 100 yards then left along North Street, right along Church Lane and first left to the teashop on the left.

Lostwithiel has a long and varied history; John Betjeman said, 'There is history in every stone', and it repays exploring. In the 13th century tin mining in Cornwall was regulated by Stannary districts. The tin was tested at the Stannary towns by cutting off a small corner or coin and so these towns, Lostwithiel, Bodmin, Truro, Liskeard, Helston and later Penzance, were also called coinage towns. Each also had its own court. Under Stannary law, a tinner was exempt from the jurisdiction of other courts. There was also a Stannary Parliament that met in Lostwithiel to protect the tinners' ancient customs and make their laws, so the town could be said to be the capital of the county. This fell into abeyance in 1752 and arches and buttresses in Quay Street are all that remain of a much grander complex of buildings that included the Coinage Hall. The town suffered badly in the Civil War. Lostwithiel and the Fowey peninsula were occupied by 10,000 Parliamentary troops. Hunger and disease were rife among the poor, civilian population. Many buildings were damaged, including the church: Royalists had taken refuge there and the Roundheads tried to dislodge them by exploding a barrel of gunpowder. Lostwithiel has also been important as a port and a centre of iron mining and tanning. In 1859 the Great Western Railway came through and Isambard Kingdom Brunel designed maintenance works, which were a significant source of employment for many years.

5. Turn left out of the teashop and follow the road down to the river. Cross the bridge to Lostwithiel station on the right. Take the train to Bodmin Parkway, the next station.

Lostwithiel grew up at the lowest bridging point of the Fowey and was an important port until mining activity further up the valley caused the anchorage to silt up. By the 15th century the river had become unnavigable to larger ships and the port moved downstream to Fowey (see Walk 17, page 83). After that, cargo was exported downriver on shallow draft boats. The bridge was originally built by the Normans and has been repaired, renewed and in constant use ever since. It has had to adapt as the river has changed course. The foundations of four more arches are under North Street and some of the eastern arches were added later.

6. Cross the line and leave the station. Turn right towards the car park. Go through a gate onto a surfaced track, signed 'Footpath to Lanhydrock House 1¾ miles'. Walk along the track lined with magnificent specimen trees. Just before a house and a gate onto a lane turn left into the car park where this walk started.

Prior to the Dissolution of the Monasteries, the Lanhydrock estate belonged to Bodmin's Augustinian priory of St Petroc. In 1620 it was acquired by the Robartes family, who had made their fortune from tin and wool, and it remained in their possession until it passed to the National Trust in 1953. The magnificent mansion, not passed on this walk, was badly damaged by fire in 1881 and was reconstructed to the same plan but incorporating every modern convenience. Not only the public rooms but also the kitchen, nursery and estate office are open to the public and give a glimpse of life in an opulent Victorian country mansion.

Walk 17
FOWEY AND POLRUAN

This walk uses two ferries and a famous path to explore the Fowey estuary, including Fowey itself and its sister community across the river, Polruan, both with a long and interesting history. The path is mainly in woodland, now owned and protected by the National Trust, but that does not prevent a series of splendid views across the estuary from being enjoyed. The route is quite energetic, with a couple of significant climbs – all the better to justify a good tea at a charming traditional teashop before the second ferry trip. All in all, this walk is a gem and highly recommended.

This charming teashop, run by three ladies from the village, is perfectly positioned as you enter Polruan and has a most friendly and obliging atmosphere. It is simple but beautifully done with many thoughtful touches, such as fresh flowers on the tables and a discreet background of light classics. They serve a selection of homemade cakes and light lunches of soup, sandwiches and baguettes. Called

'Crumpets', they of course serve these as well as toasted teacakes and saffron cake. They are open from Easter until the October half-term every day except Monday. In August, they open Monday as well. There is no telephone.

There are many alternatives in Fowey.

DISTANCE: 3½ miles.

MAP: OS Explorer 107 St Austell and Liskeard.

STARTING POINT: Caffa Mill car park (charge), Fowey (GR 126522). If this is full, use the main town car park and follow the signed path down to the town and walk through Fowey to the Bodinnick ferry.

HOW TO GET THERE: The car park is at the end of the B3269, Lostwithiel-Fowey road, signed 'Bodinnick Ferry' on the approach to Fowey.

ALTERNATIVE STARTING POINT: If you wish to visit the teashop at the beginning or end of your walk, start at Polruan, where there is a car park at the edge of the village. The teashop is in the centre of Polruan, on the road leading down to the quay. You will then start the walk at point 9.

FERRY INFORMATION: At the time of writing the Bodinnick ferry is continuous all year until 8.50pm or dusk, whichever is earlier. The Polruan ferry runs about every 15 minutes from Polruan to Whitehouse Quay during the day in summer. In winter and in the evening it runs to Town Quay, nearer the centre of Fowey. Both ferries may be suspended in adverse weather, but I doubt you would want to do the walk then!

THE WALK

1. Take the ferry across the river. Walk ahead steeply up through Bodinnick for 200 yards.

On the waterfront is 'Ferryside', once the home of author Daphne du Maurier, who did much to give Cornwall its romantic image. She was 19, hunting for a holiday home with her mother and sisters when she first came to Bodinnick – and fell instantly in love. Her parents bought Ferryside and the following year Daphne came for the first of many writing trips. Her first book, 'The Loving Spirit', was based on a boat-building family from Polruan. One of her readers was so intrigued he sailed into Fowey haven to find the author. In July 1932 she married him, sailing up the river on the morning tide to St Wyllow's church at Lanteglos. Daphne and 'Tommy', later General Sir Frederick Browning, then sailed west for a honeymoon on the Helford river and Frenchman's Creek (see Walk 13, page 65).

2. Turn right, signed 'Hall Walk Pont & Polruan'. There are many fine views from the path with seats well placed to admire them. Follow the path along the top edge of woods above Pont Pill to a gate into a field and ahead to a gate on the right.

The Hall Walk used to be known as the King's Walk. Charles I was observing the Parliamentary troops in Fowey from here and only narrowly missed being shot. A plaque by the path records the event.

3. Go through the gate and follow the path down through the woods. Follow the main path round to the right, signed 'Polruan', as a path joins on the left.

4. Cross a footbridge at the head of the creek and follow the path up the other side for 100 yards.

5. Turn right up steps, signed 'Polruan'. Follow the path through woods then up the left-hand side of a field to a stile into woods.

6. Some 20 yards after the stile the path forks: bear right, signed 'Polruan'. Ignore a path forking right, downhill, and stay on the main path as far as a lane.

7. Turn right for 25 yards then left, yet again signed 'Polruan'.

8. At the bottom of steps into the village turn right, shortly down more steps. Turn left along East Street, down a few more steps, to the teashop at crossroads.

9. With your back to the teashop turn left down to the quay and catch the ferry back to Fowey. Walk up to the road and turn right. Turn right again at a T-junction and follow the road through Fowey to the start.

Fowey (pronounced 'Foy') came to prominence as a port as the anchorage upriver at Lostwithiel started to silt up (see Walk 16, page 79). Its busy quays were alive with vessels unloading cargoes of wine, corn, timber and salt from Breton ports and returning with Cornish cloth, pilchards and tin. Fowey sailors gained a reputation for fearlessness and daring and were much in demand to man fighting ships during the Hundred Years War. In 1337 the town supplied

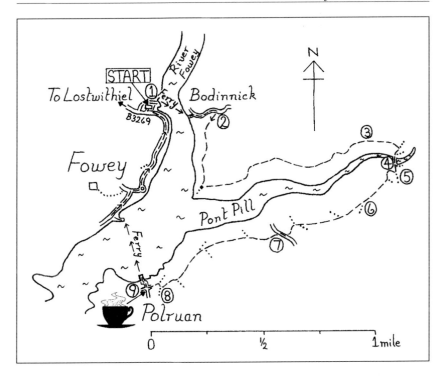

19 ships manned by 547 Fowey men and in 1346 it was the assembly point for
the siege of Calais, when 47 ships with 770 sailors on board left the port. After
the war was officially concluded, the local seamen – nicknamed the Fowey
Gallants – carried on their private vendetta against the French and made
numerous raids along the French coast and harried French shipping. In 1457
the Bretons struck back and set fire to the town. The inhabitants retreated to
Place House, the home of the Treffry family, just above the church. The defence
was organised by the formidable Dame Elizabeth Treffry, in the absence of her
husband. She is said to have poured molten lead on the raiders.

Fowey remained notorious as a haunt of pirates. One, John Wilcock, seized 15
ships off the coast of Brittany in a fortnight in 1469. Edward IV ordered the
Gallants to stop as England was by now at peace with the French but the men
of Fowey were not interested and sent the royal messenger back minus an ear
to emphasize their point. Eventually, the piracy subsided and Fowey turned to
honest trade, becoming an important port for the export of china clay in the
19th century.

Walk 18
MINIONS AND THE CHEESEWRING

This is a very short walk and not at all arduous despite exploring one of the most challenging environments in Cornwall. Nonetheless, it might well take longer than you would think to complete because there are so many interesting features. It explores one of the more accessible corners of Bodmin Moor and has a wealth of archaeological legacy, both ancient and modern, to explore. In addition, there are outstanding views from the Cheesewring so it is essential to choose a clear day.

All the moorland is privately owned and the tracks and paths used are NOT rights of way. However, the Minions Project aims to make this fascinating heritage more available to visitors, and walkers have had relatively free access for many years.

☕ The teashop at Minions is housed in the village Post Office and shop and offers hearty sustenance to hungry walkers. In particular, I welcomed the huge teapot with mugs. The sandwiches are substantial, made with bread cut from the loaf and they also serve excellent pasties. There is a small selection of delicious cakes as well as cream teas and toasted teacakes. There are some tables outside and the tearoom is behind the village shop, with a sign directing you to the sea view, which can be made out on a clear day. They are open all day, every day throughout the year. Telephone: 01579 363386.

DISTANCE: 3 miles.

MAP: OS Explorer 109 Bodmin Moor.

STARTING POINT: Minions car park to the south west of the village (GR 260711).

HOW TO GET THERE: From the A38 at Dobwalls, three miles west of Liskeard, take a minor road signed 'Common Moor Darite and St Cleer'. Follow the signs to Minions village, using the car park on the left just before the village.

ALTERNATIVE STARTING POINT: There are very few roads on Bodmin Moor so this walk differs from most in that the teashop is very close to the starting point. Therefore, there is no alternative starting point.

THE WALK

Despite the altitude and remoteness of this place, the landscape that this walk explores has been heavily influenced by human activity. Before man had any impact the moor was probably lightly wooded. There have been essentially three phases of human activity. In the Bronze Age, 3,500 years ago, this area was farmed and there are traces of field systems and huts scattered across the moor. There was also some tin extracted. Britain was famous for its tin and Phoenician merchants visited these islands even then for this valuable metal. In those far-off days the climate was somewhat more benign than it is now, though even then farming was probably marginal. The farms were abandoned as the climate became harsher and Cornwall has never been farmed again on the same scale. The next wave was the mining and quarrying boom of the 19th century, which left major scars on the landscape, and this has been followed by the third wave, of which you are part, tourists coming to see the relics of the past.

1. Leave the car park up steps at the left rear and go ahead to a track. Turn right. The Hurlers are on the right of the track. After inspecting them return to the track and continue along it for half a mile.

The Hurlers are three stone circles that were constructed about 3,500 years ago, during the Bronze Age. We may never know the significance of these or other stone circles (see Walk 10, page 54).

2. At a three-way junction the main route lies to the right but it is worth diverting left for half a mile to another stone circle and a closer look at the disused Gold Diggings Quarry. This, believe it or not, is a popular picnic spot: you will see why when you get there!

To visit Craddock Moor stone circle turn left off the track and go towards Gold Diggings Quarry as the track turns right. Walk across a low mound covered in bracken; this is an ancient burial mound. Head towards a prominent tor, Tregarrick Tor, for 200 yards.

The stone circle is not at all obvious. It consists of 15 stones, all now fallen. It is one of many dotted across the moors. Bronze Age field systems and hut circles have been detected in this area.

Return to the junction and take what would have been the right branch. Ignore a path on the left and continue towards the Cheesewring, an obvious rocky tor, to a junction of five paths.

Rock containing tin ore is eroded from the mother lode and transported by streams forming what is known as an alluvial deposit. The path crosses an area where such a deposit has been worked. This can be recognised by the unevenness of the ground caused by its being dug over to find the ore.

3. From here make your way to the Cheesewring and the summit: left then right after 140 yards is an easy way.

Bodmin Moor is a boss of granite that pushed up from deep within the earth about 280 million years ago. This granite is the backbone of the southwest peninsula from Dartmoor to the Scilly Isles. Fissures in the rock expose surfaces to the weathering agents of the environment such as water and wind and the degraded material is then transported out leaving a pile of more resistant rock. Sometimes the top stone becomes so weathered it can be rocked; this is known as a loggan stone (see Walk 9, page 47). It is said that the top stone of the Cheesewring could be rocked with a pole, but this is no longer the case. The Cheesewring is just the best known example of a phenomenon found all over the

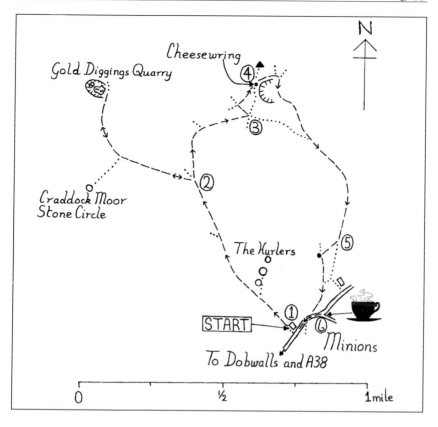

moors, *as can be seen from the other examples on the summit. The upper surfaces have rounded depressions that early antiquarians thought were 'Druidical' but are now known to be formed by the action of water at weak points.*

The Cheesewring was supposed to be the haunt of a druid who had a golden cup that never ran dry and provided thirsty passers-by with an endless supply of water. What the truth behind this story was we shall never know but, interestingly, a skeleton clutching a gold cup was found in a nearby burial chamber. Known as the Rillaton Cup it was given to William IV. Apparently George V used it to keep his collar studs in before it was given to the British Museum.

4. After exploring the summit return to a point with the Cheesewring on your right and the fence at the edge of the quarry in front of you.

Follow the fence down to your left. This is steep but shortly reaches a track. Turn right into and through the quarry and continue along the track. (An alternative route that avoids the steep decent is to return to point 3 and turn left.)

The fine, silver grey granite extracted from here was used in many construction projects, including docks from Birkenhead to Copenhagen, and Tower Bridge. At its height in the 1860s over 100 men and boys were employed here. If you look at the rock face you can see the joints and fissures that allow the weathering described above. You will probably see rock-climbers too as this face is very popular, with many technically challenging routes.

Outside the southwest corner of the quarry is Daniel Gumb's cave. He was an 18th-century mathematician and philosopher who earned his living as a stonecutter and surveyor. He lived in a stone house with his wife and several children. It stood where the quarry is now and this is a partial reconstruction. Note the geometrical carving on the roof.

All around is evidence of the mining boom of the 19th century. As the granite intrusion cooled, hot fluids and gases deposited metal ores, notably copper and tin, in fissures. This metal had been worked in a small way since prehistoric times but the introduction of steam technology allowed the scale of this to increase dramatically until the industry was destroyed by falling prices. The Phoenix United mine to the left of the track was once the largest in Cornwall. It employed over 600 men and women and produced 16,000 tons of tin and 83,000 tons of copper.

5. Bear right to an engine house, which now houses Minions Heritage Centre. This is free and puts all you have seen into context. Take the track from the Heritage Centre into the village and the teashop across the road to the left.

Minions is the highest village in Cornwall. The success of the mines brought hundreds of miners and their families: women and girls were employed to sort the ore at the surface. Most of the buildings date from that time. As the industry collapsed, the miners left to find employment elsewhere.

6. Turn left out of the teashop along the main road back to the start.

Walk 19
CALSTOCK AND COTEHELE

*T*he river Tamar, which separates Cornwall from Devon, had many quays along its tidal reaches. They have been superseded by modern transport but are an interesting reminder of former trade. This walk visits two of them and the route between is an attractive mixture of woods, fields and quiet lanes. After tea at Cotehele Quay the return is through woodland and climbs up the side of the valley to avoid the marshes fringing the river. If you wish, and the tide is right, you can return to Calstock by ferry along the river. This makes a most enjoyable finale to a pleasant walk. (Telephone 01822 83333).

 The tearoom at Cotehele Quay is housed in an 18th-century building. Originally a lime-burner's cottage, it had become a public house by 1832 and so it remained until the early 20th century. After that it was a private house until it became a tearoom in 1980. It has a pretty garden to one side and offers the excellent fare we have come to expect from the National Trust tearooms. They are open every day from late March until the end of October from 11 am until 5 pm (noon until 6 pm on Sunday) and also on Sundays in November and December. Downstairs is a traditional tearoom serving a delicious selection of cakes and cream teas, which you can supplement with a choice of filled rolls. Upstairs is more of a bistro, which serves a range of hot and cold meals. Telephone: 01579 350024.

When the teashop is closed there are pubs in Calstock and Lower Metherell, passed on the route.

DISTANCE: 5½ miles.
MAP: OS Explorer 108 Lower Tamar Valley and Plymouth.
STARTING POINT: Calstock village car park (GR 437684).
HOW TO GET THERE: Calstock is signed from the A390, Liskeard-Tavistock road, near Drakewalls. Drive through Calstock to the main car park beyond the quay.
ALTERNATIVE STARTING POINT: If you wish to visit the teashop at the beginning or end of your walk, start at Cotehele Quay, where there is a large car park (National Trust, charge for non-members). You will then start the walk at point 11.

THE WALK

Calstock was a thriving port in the 19th century, exporting tin and copper ores and granite. The area was also famed for its market gardens, producing fruit and flowers on the warm hillsides. The village was a favourite destination for paddle steamers and thousands of day-trippers used to come from Plymouth and Devonport; so much so that the local clergy felt they had to remonstrate about the evils of pleasure trips on the Sabbath.

1. Go to the riverbank and turn right along the quay. At the end of the quay follow the road uphill to the right to a T-junction. Turn left for 45 yards then bear left along Lower Kelly, signed 'Cotehele 1¼'.

2. Just before Calstock Boatyard turn right on a signed path that climbs up the side of the valley for about 600 yards to a fork.

3. Bear left, initially downhill and under a footbridge, to meet a track.

4. Turn right. When the track forks by a ruined building after a third of a mile, bear left. Continue ahead when a major path joins on the left to walk with a stream on the left to a lane.

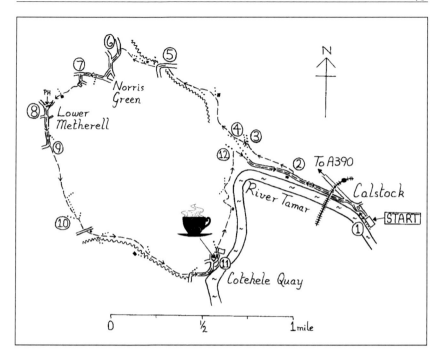

5. Turn left for 45 yards then, when the lane bends sharp left, continue ahead along a track, signed 'Mill'. Ignore a track on the right after 10 yards. Soon after passing the ruined mill bear left and follow the path uphill through woods then along the left-hand side of a field to a lane.

6. Turn left. At a T-junction turn left into Norris Green. After 70 yards fork right, signed 'Metherell Harrowbarrow'. At the next T-junction turn right for 250 yards.

7. Turn left along Nicholas Meadow for 70 yards then turn right. After 45 yards continue ahead on a path, signed 'Lower Metherell ¼'. After passing through a gate press on along the right hand side of a field then ahead along a track. At the entrance to Brooklands continue in the same direction, now on a path, and again go ahead when it becomes a lane in the village. When this forks, bear left.

8. At a T-junction turn left.

9. When the road bends sharp right continue in the same direction on a signed path up the left hand side of a field. When the hedge on the left ends, keep on in the same direction to a stile then ahead, now with a wood on the left to a surfaced track.

☕ **10.** Turn left to a lane. Cross the lane and go through a gate onto a track, passing Orchard Cottage to reach a river. Continue with the river on your right, ignoring all paths to left and right. At a lane continue ahead to Cotehele Quay and the teashop.

The Edgcumbe family built Cotehele House, not passed on this route, between 1485 and 1539. Soon afterwards they built another house across the water from Plymouth (see Walk 20, page 94).

11. Turn left out of the tearoom. At the entrance to the car park bear left onto a track and follow this uphill. Pass a chapel on the right and continue downhill to a T-junction.

During the Wars of the Roses in the 15th century the Edgcumbes supported the Lancastrian cause. When the Yorkist forces of Richard III came to arrest Richard Edgcumbe he managed to escape into the woods. He threw his hat, weighted with a stone, into the river and fooled the pursuing men into thinking he had leapt to his death. He went on to fight for Henry VII at Bosworth Field and was knighted for his contribution. He built this chapel in thanksgiving for his escape.

12. Turn right. Continue ahead when the track becomes a lane to rejoin the outward route and retrace your steps back to the start.

The massive twelve-span viaduct towers 120 feet above Calstock. It was opened in 1907 and was one of the first to be built of concrete blocks. Its construction proved to be a difficult project, running over time and budget. The railway line sounded the death knell of Calstock's traditional trade and still carries trains from Plymouth to Gunnislake on the beautiful Tamar Valley line.

(If you started at Cotehele Quay and do not wish to visit Calstock, turn left at point 2, just after Calstock boatyard.)

Walk 20
MOUNT EDGCUMBE

This highly recommended walk lies as far southeast as it is possible to be in Cornwall, just a short ferry hop from Plymouth in Devon. It explores the coast and countryside round Mount Edgcumbe, the ancestral home of the Edgcumbe family and now managed as a country park by Cornwall County Council and Plymouth City Council. Much of the outward leg is through mature woodland yet beside the sea, an unusual and pleasant experience. Other highlights of this route are the fantastic views across the Sound and the gardens of Mount Edgcumbe, in which the tearoom is situated. They are freely open to the public and well worth taking the time to explore.

The route as described starts on the spine of the peninsula. It begins by dropping down to the coast path on one side and ends by climbing up from the river on the other. This means that the main ascent is at the very end of the walk, when you might be a bit tired, despite a good tea. The alternative start in Cremyll, inevitable if you are coming by ferry from Plymouth, has much to recommend it.

☕ The Orangery in the formal garden is a Grade II listed building and now houses a very comfortable tearoom with a beautiful outlook. There is an excellent selection of delicious cakes and, of course, they serve cream teas. For lunch a tasty choice of filled baguettes or jacket potatoes or pasties is offered together with soup. There is also a special children's menu. They are open all year from 10.30 am until 5.30 pm every day. Telephone 01752 822586.

DISTANCE: 4½ miles.

MAP: OS Explorer 108 Lower Tamar Valley and Plymouth.

STARTING POINT: Car park at Maker church (GR 447520).

HOW TO GET THERE: From the A374, which leads from the A38 to Torpoint, take the B3247 and follow the road through Millbrook towards Cremyll. About two miles past Millbrook take a drive on the right that leads to the car park beyond the church.

ALTERNATIVE STARTING POINT: If you wish to visit the teashop at the beginning or end of your walk, start in Cremyll where there is a car park (charge). The teashop is across the road, through the gates and to the left, under an arch. An alternative way to get to this walk is to take the Cremyll ferry from Plymouth. You will then start the walk at point 3.

THE WALK

At 400 feet above sea level, the mainly 15th-century Maker church is in a panoramic position. This led to an unusual use in the 18th century, when it was pressed into service as a signal tower during the Napoleonic Wars.

1. With your back to the church turn right through a gate in the right-hand corner of the car park and follow the track as it loops down and round to the left. At a fork bear right to continue gently downhill. Keep ahead as the coast path, waymarked by an acorn symbol, joins on the right, shortly passing Picklecombe Seat. When the way ahead is barred by a fence, go up steps on the left then follow the path as it zigzags up the cliff, following the waymarks. Now follow the path down again. At the bottom of the first set of steps, cross a track and continue down further steps. This diversion is to avoid a landslip.

The Mount Edgcumbe estate was bought by Plymouth City Council and Cornwall District Council in 1971 and turned into a country park. The park covers some 865 acres and has been famous since it was created in the 18th

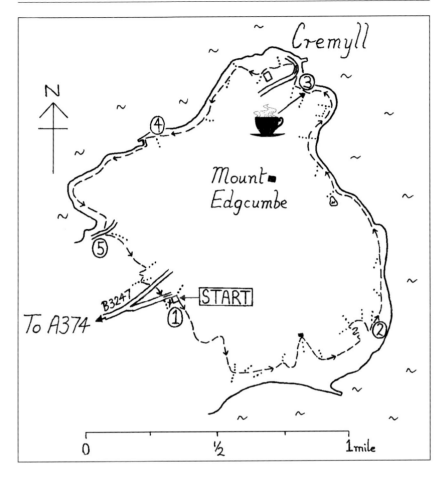

century by the first Earl of Mount Edgcumbe, who was an Admiral of the Fleet. Scattered throughout the park are buildings, deliberately sited to create vistas and provide atmosphere.

2. Some 80 yards after reaching the far side of the landslip fork right, indicated by a yellow waymark on a post, and follow the coast path down to and beside the shore. This passes through a deer gate into the gardens. Continue beside the shore. Go into the Historic Gardens and still keep on the path beside the shore. This eventually leads to the formal garden overlooked by the Orangery, housing the tearoom.

There is a good view of Plymouth breakwater from the path. It was constructed to protect the Sound against the heavy sea swell that rolls in from the southwest and was constructed between 1811 and 1841. It took four and a half million tons of local limestone. There are beacon lights at both ends and a refuge at the eastern side up which survivors from a wreck can climb and await rescue.

The Historic Gardens, a Grade I listed monument, are well worth taking a little time to explore. Go up the steps at the back of the Italian Garden overlooked by the Orangery. Orange trees are taken out into the garden in the summer but protected inside the building in winter, as was intended. Originally a 17th-century wilderness garden, the gardens were laid out in the 18th century but are not just a period piece. The modern American and New Zealand gardens, the latter with geyser, reflect Edgcumbe family connections.

3. Leave the gardens via the arch and go ahead on a path to a gate on the right, looking left for a view of Edgcumbe House. Follow the path to a road. Turn right and shortly take a track on the left, signed 'Empacombe ¾' passing the public conveniences. Ignore a track on the right. When the track bends left by a car park, turn right to continue on the signed path.

In 1493 Piers Edgcumbe from Cotehele (see Walk 19, page 92) married Jean Darnford, an heiress with considerable estates both sides of the Tamar. Sir Piers created a deer park and the first house was started in 1547. The family moved their household here in the late 17th century. A stray bomb from the raids on Plymouth in 1941 seriously damaged the house, which was restored by the sixth earl between 1958 and 1964.

4. Continue ahead when the path joins a surfaced drive to shortly go through a gap in a low wall. Turn left and walk round the edge of the quay to a stile. Cross the stile and follow the path along the shore to a lane.

5. Take a path on the opposite side of the lane, signed; 'Maker church ½ Kingsand 1¼'. The path does not go along the obvious track but to the right of it, up a grassy slope, to a fence corner, then ahead to a gate into a wood. Follow the signed path as it zigzags up through the wood to a road. Cross the road to continue on the path to a track. Turn left back to the car park.